# OCR Level 3 ITQ

## Unit 32
## Desktop Publishing Software

## Using
## Microsoft® Publisher 2007

Release ITQOCR48v1

*Published by:*

        CiA Training Ltd

        Business & Innovation Centre

        Sunderland Enterprise Park

        Sunderland

        SR5 2TA

        United Kingdom


        Tel:     +44 (0) 191 549 5002

        Fax:    +44 (0) 191 549 9005


        E-mail:  info@ciatraining.co.uk

        Web:    www.ciatraining.co.uk


        **ISBN:**   **978-1-86005-930-8**

---

## Important Notes

This guide was written for *Microsoft Office 2007* running on *Windows 7*. If using a different version of *Windows* some dialog boxes may look and function slightly differently to that described. It is also assumed file extensions are enabled in *Windows*, which is important for demonstrating the differences between file types.

To turn on file extensions, click the **Start** button and open the **Control Panel**. From **Appearance and Personalization** select **Folder Options**, and then from the dialog box click the **View** tab and uncheck **Hide extensions for known file types**. Click **OK**.

A resolution of *1024x768* was also used to produce screenshots for this guide. Working at a different resolution (or with an application window which is not maximised) may change the look of the menus and toolbars, which change to fit the space available.

---

*First published 2010*

## Overview of the unit

This level 3 unit is called **Desktop Publishing Software** and requires you to use suitable software to combine and manipulate text, images and graphics to create publications that will be suitable for screen or print. It has a credit value of **5**.

At this level you are required to demonstrate the skills and techniques necessary to use a wide range of advanced publishing tools to produce publications that are at times non-routine or unfamiliar.

This guide is designed to be used with *Microsoft Publisher 2007* and contains exercises covering the following topics:

- Publishing Basics
- Publication Design
- Opening Publications
- Saving Publications
- Creating Publications
- Entering Text
- Editing and Formatting Text

- Formatting Text Boxes
- Inserting Pictures
- Drawing Shapes
- Manipulating Pictures
- Combining Text and Pictures
- Creating Web Publications
- Checking Publications

## Software and data files

*Microsoft Publisher 2007* is part of the *Microsoft Office 2007* suite of applications. This guide assumes that the program has been fully installed on your computer. Some features described in this guide may not work correctly if the program was not fully installed.

Downloadable data accompanying this guide contains files to enable you to practise new techniques without the need for data entry. Newly created files can be saved to the same location.

---

### Downloading the Data Files

The data files associated with this guide must be downloaded from our website. To do this, go to **www.ciatraining.co.uk/data** and follow the simple on-screen instructions.

Your *FastCode* for this guide's data is: **ITQOCR48**

The data will be installed to the following location in your **Documents** library\folder:

**DATA FILES \ OCR Level 3 ITQ \ Unit 32 Publisher 2007**

If you prefer, the data files can also be supplied on CD at an additional cost. Contact the Sales team at info@ciatraining.co.uk.

---

## Aims and objectives

The purpose of this guide is to provide the knowledge and techniques necessary to meet the learning outcomes and assessment criteria for this optional unit.

After completing this guide you will be able to:

- Understand Publishing Basics
- Recognise design features
- Use *Publisher* to create new publications
- Create text boxes and add text from a variety of sources
- Format text and text boxes
- Insert and manipulate pictures
- Draw and manipulate shapes
- Combine pictures and text
- Arrange objects on a page
- Create Web Publications

## Notation used throughout this guide

- Key presses are included within angled brackets. For example, **<Enter>** means press the **Enter** key.

- Menu selections are written in the form **File | Open**, meaning select the **File** option and then **Open** from the submenu that appears.

- The guide is split into individual exercises. Each exercise usually consists of a written explanation of a specific learning outcome (Knowledge), followed by a stepped exercise (Activity).

## Recommendations

- Work through the exercises in sequence so that one feature is understood before moving on to the next.

- Read the whole of each exercise before starting to work through it. This ensures understanding of the topic and prevents unnecessary mistakes.

## This guide is suitable for:

- Any individual wishing to gain the skills necessary to produce ITQ (2009) evidence for this unit. The user should work through the guide from start to finish.

- Tutor led groups as reinforcement material. It can be used as and when necessary.

# Skill Check

After you have finished working through each Skill Set, come back to this checklist and review your progress. You judge when you are competent – only when you fully understand the learning aims of each exercise topic should you progress to the next Skill Set.

**1**: No Knowledge **2**: Some Knowledge  **3**: Competent

| Skill Set | No | Exercise | 1 | 2 | 3 |
|---|---|---|---|---|---|
| **1 Basics** | 1 | Desktop Publishing | | | |
| | 2 | The *Publisher* Screen | | | |
| | 3 | The Publication Page | | | |
| | 4 | Opening a Publication | | | |
| | 5 | Basic Layout | | | |
| | 6 | Saving a Publication | | | |
| **2 Creating Publications** | 8 | Creating a Blank Publication | | | |
| | 9 | Layout Guides | | | |
| | 10 | Importing Text Files | | | |
| | 11 | Text Overflow | | | |
| | 12 | Linked Text Boxes | | | |
| | 13 | Alternative Text Entry | | | |
| | 14 | Editing text | | | |
| **3 Text Formatting** | 16 | Simple Formatting | | | |
| | 17 | Styles | | | |
| | 18 | Text Box Formatting | | | |
| | 19 | Columns | | | |
| **4 Pictures** | 21 | Image Files | | | |
| | 22 | Importing Images from Devices | | | |
| | 23 | Clip Art | | | |
| | 24 | WordArt | | | |
| | 25 | Shapes | | | |
| | 26 | Combining Shapes | | | |
| | 27 | Text Wrapping | | | |
| | 28 | Position and Size | | | |

# Skill Check

**1**: No Knowledge **2**: Some Knowledge  **3**: Competent

| **5 Other Objects** | 30 | Tables | | | |
|---|---|---|---|---|---|
| | 31 | Objects from Files | | | |
| | 32 | Linked Objects | | | |
| | 33 | Hyperlinks | | | |

| **6 Multiple Page Layout** | 35 | Multiple Pages | | | |
|---|---|---|---|---|---|
| | 36 | Master Pages | | | |
| | 37 | Headers and Footers | | | |

| **7 Web Publications** | 39 | Creating Web Pages | | | |
|---|---|---|---|---|---|
| | 40 | Navigation Links | | | |
| | 41 | Hyperlinks | | | |
| | 42 | Animations | | | |
| | 43 | Sounds | | | |
| | 44 | Web Page Preview | | | |
| | 45 | Save As Web Page | | | |
| | 46 | Web Site Template | | | |

| **8 Design** | 48 | Practical Publications | | | |
|---|---|---|---|---|---|
| | 49 | Design Styles | | | |
| | 50 | Colour Schemes | | | |
| | 51 | Font Schemes | | | |
| | 52 | Layout | | | |
| | 53 | Business Information | | | |

| **9 Finishing** | 55 | Creating Templates | | | |
|---|---|---|---|---|---|
| | 56 | Print Setup | | | |
| | 57 | Printing | | | |
| | 58 | Publication Checking | | | |
| | 59 | File Types | | | |
| | 60 | Save as Picture | | | |
| | 61 | File Type Considerations | | | |

# Contents

# Skill Set 1

# Basics

By the end of this Skill Set you should be able to:

Understand *Publisher* Basics

Start *Publisher*

Use Preset Templates

Recognise the *Publisher* Screen

Open and Close a Publication

Save a Publication

Close *Publisher*

# Exercise 1 - Desktop Publishing

### *Knowledge:*

Desktop publishing applications such as *Microsoft Publisher* were originally designed to allow professional quality printed documents to be produced on your own computer without the need to employ specialist publishing services. The documents often produced were those that relied heavily on layout and impact rather than just content, such as posters, brochures and newsletters. Currently, the output of desktop publishing is just as likely to be viewed on a screen, either as part of a multimedia production or as a web page on the Internet or local intranet.

As word processing applications have developed, they now handle many features that would once have required a desktop publishing solution. Both applications can be used to produce documents of a high quality, but in general, desktop publishing specialises in highly visual layout combining text, graphics and other elements.

Each item within a publication, e.g. a picture, table or text frame, is known as an **object**. Desktop publishing applications allow you to work with text, pictures and other objects, moving and resizing them with more control over their precise positioning and layout on the page.

*Microsoft Publisher* provides many different templates to help with creating new publications. A **template** is a publication layout created for a particular purpose. It normally consists of a framework of styles, colours, graphical elements, etc. and only requires your specific content to be added.

### *Activity:*

1.  Click the **Start** button from your desktop. Locate and select **Microsoft Office Publisher 2007**. It may be available from the **Start** menu or by clicking **All Programs** and **Microsoft Office**.

2.  *Publisher* will start and the opening **Getting Started** window will be displayed.

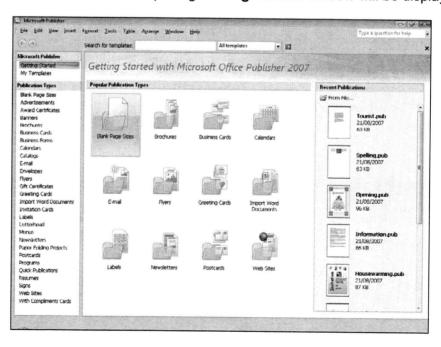

# Exercise 1 - Continued

3.  A list of available preset templates is at the left under **Publication Types**. Example templates of the currently selected **Publication Type** are shown in the centre (**Popular Publication Types** are shown on opening the window). At the right, any publications that have been opened recently will be displayed (there may not be any visible on your screen).

> **Note:** *The advantages of using a Publisher template, is that they are usually professionally designed so that the use of colour and form will be aesthetically pleasing, and also that all publications created from the same template will have a consistent look.*

4.  Select **Newsletters** from the list of **Publication Types** at the left. Various newsletter templates are shown in the central area.

5.  Click on the **Modular** design from **Newer Designs** category.

6.  The selected template is displayed in more detail at the right, where it can be customised if desired. Make no changes at the moment, but click [ Create ] at the bottom right of the window. A new publication is created.

7.  Look the **Title Bar** at the top of the window. This shows the name of the current publication (**Publication1**), the name of the application (**Microsoft Publisher**) and the expected output format, **Print Publication**.

> **Note:** *It is not the template itself that is opened, but a new publication based on the selected template. The position of objects on the page, the colours used, and the pictures, are all supplied by the template.*

8.  The publication is now available for editing. You will need to edit the content to suit your own requirements, but this will certainly be easier than starting from a blank publication. For now, leave the publication on screen and move to the next exercise.

# Exercise 2 - The Publisher Screen

### Knowledge:

All tasks involved with creating and modifying publications are carried out from the main *Publisher* editing screen.

### Activity:

1.  Look at the *Publisher* screen showing the newly created publication.

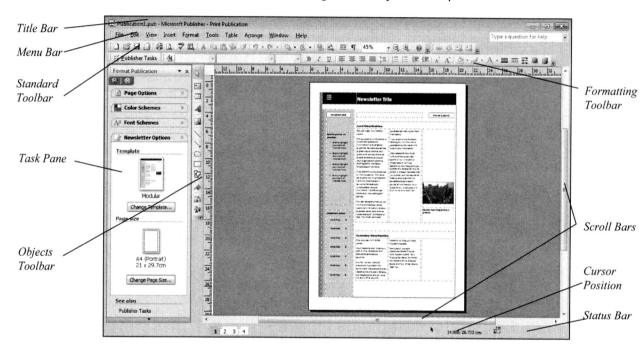

2.  Look below the **Title Bar** to see the **Menu Bar**. All of the commands necessary to use *Publisher* are contained within these menus.

3.  Look below the **Menu Bar**, to see the **Toolbars**. There are many different toolbars available although some of them will only appear when needed or specifically requested (and may appear in different locations).

4.  Look at the left of the screen to see the **Task Pane**. This area contains more controls to help with specific tasks. There are different task panes to deal with different tasks, or the task pane can be hidden. The current task pane is **Format Publication**

5.  To hide the task pane click the **Close** button, ☒, on the right of the task pane heading.

6.  Click **View** on the **Menu Bar**, then click on **Task Pane** from the menu to display the task pane again.

---

*Note:* *Some people prefer to work with the task pane hidden, as it allows more space to view the page. This guide assumes the task pane is displayed.*

---

# Exercise 2 - Continued

7.  Look between the **Task Pane** and the page display area to see the **Objects** toolbar (sometimes found on the left of the task pane). This is displayed vertically and contains tools to create and control various objects on the page.

8.  Select **View | Toolbars** to see a list of the available toolbars and which are currently displayed. Click away from the menus to remove the list.

9.  Look on the left of the **Status Bar**, located along the bottom of the window. This indicates that the current display is page **1** of a four page publication.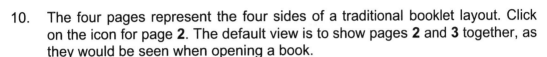

10. The four pages represent the four sides of a traditional booklet layout. Click on the icon for page **2**. The default view is to show pages **2** and **3** together, as they would be seen when opening a book.

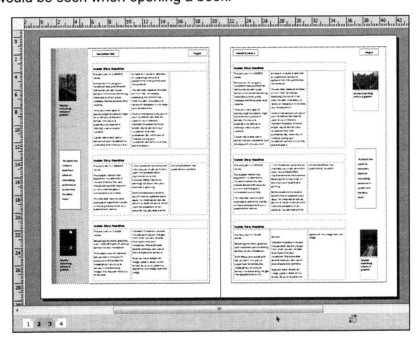

11. Display the **View** menu. The **Two-Page Spread** option should be selected. Click the option to deselect it. Now each page will be shown singly.

12. Select **View | Two-Page Spread** again to view pages 2 and 3 together again.

13. On the right of the **Status Bar** is a display showing the exact position of the cursor or the exact location and size of the currently selected object. Move the cursor to blank area of the page to see the exact cursor coordinates.

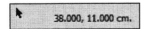

14. Clicking on any picture show its exact location and size. Click on the skyscraper picture in the top right of page 3, for example.

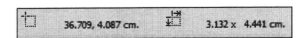

15. Leave the publication open for the next exercise.

# Exercise 3 - The Publication Page

### Knowledge:

All publication pages are made up of a collection of different objects. An object can be a box containing text or imported data records. It can be a table of numbers or a picture or a graphical shape. A simple publication may consist of two or three objects, and a complex publication may have hundreds, but the principles of manipulating the objects are the same.

Publications which are designed to be viewed can also include sound and animation objects.

### Activity:

1.  Switch back to view page **1** of **Publication1**.

2.  From the **View** menu, make sure **Boundaries and Guides** is <u>not</u> selected. The page is now shown as it would be printed.

3.  Click **View** and click **Boundaries and Guides** again so that it is selected.

> ✔  <u>B</u>oundaries and Guides

4.  Notice now that all blue layout guides are shown, and all of the objects on the page have dotted line frames, indicating their positions.

> **Note:** *Make sure that the **Boundaries and Guides** option is always selected unless specifically instructed to switch it off. This makes it much easier to arrange objects on the page.*

5.  Move the cursor over the text **Newsletter Date** in the top left of the page. A small caption (**ScreenTip**) appears, 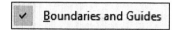. The text is contained in an object called a **Text Box**. In this example the text box has an orange border.

6.  Press the <**F9**> key to zoom in and see the detail more clearly.

> **Note:** *Zoom can be controlled more exactly by selecting settings from the **Zoom** drop down box* `100%  ▼`*, on the **Standard** toolbar.*

7.  Click on the text. The text box is now selected, which is indicated by the small white circles, known as "handles" around it. Selected objects can be moved and resized. Text can only be entered or edited in a box that is selected.

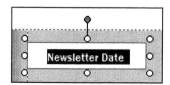

8.  With the text selected, type today's date in the format **01/12/2010**. This replaces the existing text.

# Exercise 3 - Continued

9.    Move the cursor down slightly to a blank part of the blue. The **ScreenTip** indicates that this is a **Rectangle** object. This is a special example of an object which has been drawn on the page.

10.    Click once to select the whole rectangle and press **<F9>** to zoom back out. Notice that the rectangle is almost the full height of the page and has other objects showing on top of it. Press **<F9>** to zoom in again.

11.    Move the cursor down over the blue panel to the text **Special points of interest**. The **ScreenTip** indicates that this is another **Text Box** object. Click to select it and see its extent.

12.    Move the cursor down over the blue panel to the text **Inside Story**. The **ScreenTip** indicates that this is a **Table** object. This is similar to a text box but holds information in a table structure of rows and columns.

13.    Click on the image of skyscrapers on the right of the page. The **ScreenTip** indicates that this is a **Picture** object.

**Note:**   *When a picture is selected, the **Picture** toolbar is displayed. By default this toolbar 'floats' on the screen and can be dragged to a new location.*

14.    Click **File** on the **Menu Bar** then select **Close** from the list (menu). This publication has not yet been saved so a dialog box is displayed asking if you need to save the publication.

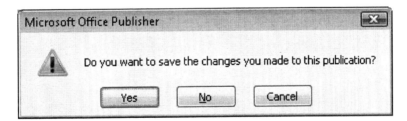

15.    Click **No**. The publication is closed without a copy being saved.

**Note:**   *If you selected **Yes**, the **Save As** box would be displayed, allowing you to name the publication and save it for later use. Saving is covered in a later exercise. **Cancel** would return to the publication without closing or saving.*

# Exercise 4 - Opening a Publication

### Knowledge:

Publications can be stored as saved files on your computer or network. To open a saved publication, simply use *Publisher's* **Open** command to locate and select the appropriate file. Alternatively, you can double-click the file in *Windows Explorer* to open it automatically in *Publisher*.

### Activity:

1.   Before starting this exercise, check that you know the location of the data files for **Unit 32** (see note on page **3**). From the **Getting Started** window select **File | Open**. The **Open Publication** dialog box is displayed.

> *Note:*   The **Open Publication** dialog box can also be displayed by clicking the **Open** button on the **Standard** toolbar, or by clicking **From File** beneath **Recent Publications** at the right of the **Getting Started** window.

2.   The default location for files in the dialog box is the **Documents** library/folder. A **DATA FILES** folder should be listed in the view area on the right. Double click on **DATA FILES** to display the contents of that folder.

3.   Double click on **OCR ITQ Level 3**, and finally on **Unit 32 Publisher 2007**. The contents of the data folder will be displayed.

> *Note:*   Depending on the version of Windows that you are using, the dialog box you see may appear slightly different to that shown above.

4.   Select the publication **Basic** and then click the **Open** button. The publication is opened. Leave it open for the next exercise.

# Exercise 5 - Basic Layout

### Knowledge:

The basic layout of a page can easily be changed by moving and resizing any of the component objects.

### Activity:

1.  Select the text box in the **Basic** publication. Click the middle handle on the right edge of the box, and drag it to the left until the box is about **9cm** wide. Use the information on the **Task Bar** to help with this.

2.  The text no longer fits in the box. Select **Format | AutoFit Text | Best Fit**. Until this is cancelled, the text in this box will always be resized automatically to be fully displayed and as large as possible.

3.  Drag the middle handle on the bottom edge of the box, and drag it to down until the box is about **4cm** high.

4.  Click on the **Triangle** shape and drag the top right handle up and right until the object size is about **6cm** wide by **9cm** high. Notice that the handle can be dragged in any direction, which can change the original shape proportion.

5.  Click on the **Planet** picture and drag the lower left handle down and left until the object is shown as about **9cm** high. Notice that however you drag the corner handle for a picture, the original proportion remains fixed.

> **Note:** *Holding down the* **<Shift>** *key whilst dragging a corner handle, will <u>always</u> retain proportion for <u>any</u> object.*

6.  Select the text box and move the cursor over one of the edges (not on a handle). Click and drag the box to near the middle of the page.

7.  Click and drag the triangle and the picture to create the following effect.

> **Note:** *The 'order' of objects was already correct for this example. Changing order is covered in a later exercise.*

8.  Leave the publication open for the next exercise.

# Exercise 6 - Saving a Publication

### Knowledge:

Any publication must be saved if it is to be used again. There are two main ways to save a document: **Save As** and **Save**. **Save As** creates a new file and requires a file name, file type and location to be specified. It is therefore always used to save a newly created publication. When a publication has already been saved, **Save** can be used to update the current changes in the original file.

### Activity:

1. The publication **Basic** has been altered and there is a choice of saving methods. **Save** will overwrite the original **Basic** file, and **Save As** will create a new file. Select **File | Save As**.

> **Note:** *For a new, unsaved publication, the* **Save** *or* **Save As** *options will both display the* **Save As** *dialog box.*

2. The **Save As** dialog box should display the contents of the supplied data folder, if not, locate it now (see exercise 4 for more information).

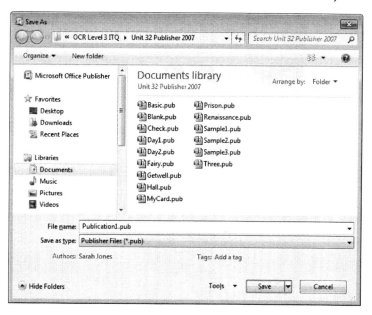

3. Enter **modified** in the **File name** box.

4. Click the drop down arrow in the box where the file type of the saved file is set and look at the selections available.

5. Leave setting as the default **Publisher Files (*.pub)** and click the **Save** button, ⌷ Save ▼ .

6. The publication is saved as a new file publisher file named **modified**.

7. Select **File | Close** to close the publication.

8. Select **File | Exit** to close the *Publisher* application.

# Exercise 7 - Develop Your Skills

You will find a *Develop Your Skills* exercise at the end of each Skill Set. Work through it to ensure you've understood the previous exercises.

1.   Start *Publisher*.

2.   Use the **Getting Started** window to create a **Newsletter** type of publication based on the **Marker** design.

3.   How many pages are there in this publication?

4.   Name 2 items that appear along the top of the *Publisher* window.

5.   Name 2 items that appear down the left of the *Publisher* window.

6.   Save the publication as **skills** and close it. Leave *Publisher* open.

7.   Open the publication **Renaissance** which can be found in the supplied data folder.

8.   How many pages are there in this publication?

9.   Set the **Zoom** setting so that the whole page can be seen.

10.   Set the **Zoom** setting to **75%**.

11.   Use any method to remove the **Task Pane** from the left of the screen.

12.   Use a **Menu** option to display the **Task Pane** again.

13.   Display page **3** of the publication and click on the word **Conclusion**. From the information on the screen, what size is the text box that contains this word?

14.   By dragging a handle of this text box, change its height to **10cm**, without changing its width.

15.   A picture overlaps this text box. Is any of the text hidden?

16.   Close the publication <u>without</u> saving.

17.   **Exit** *Publisher*.

---

| Note: | The answers are listed in the **Answers** section at the end of the guide. |
|-------|----------------------------------------------------------------------------|

# Summary: Basics

In this Skill Set you have seen some of the basic principles of publications. You have seen how to start and close *Publisher*, and have been introduced to some of the main features of the *Publisher* screens.

You have also seen how to start a new publication based on the many existing templates and styles available, how to open an existing publication, and how to close down individual publications and the *Publisher* application.

Many of the skills in this Skill Set are essential basic skills which are needed to perform any publisher activities.

Your OCR ITQ evidence must demonstrate your ability to:

- Start and close the *Publisher* application

- Start and close standard publications

- Open and close existing applications

# Skill Set 2

# Creating Publications

By the end of this Skill Set you should be able to:

Create Publications

Use Layout Guides

Create Text Boxes

Link Text Boxes

Import Text Files

Use Alternative Text Entry

Edit Text

# Exercise 8 - Creating a Blank Publication

### Knowledge:

Although it is usually recommended for beginners to base their publications on the **Templates** that are provided in *Publisher*, it is useful to know how to create a publication from scratch. Blank publications can be easily created from the **Getting Started** window.

### Activity:

1.  Start *Publisher* to display the **Getting Started** screen.

> **Note:** *This screen can be displayed at any time by selecting **File | New**.*

2.  Select the **Blank Page Sizes** option from the main panel (or from the list at the left). This displays all of the different sizes of blank publication available.

Blank Page Sizes

3.  Scroll down the display to see the range of blank sizes grouped into a variety of categories such as **Standard**, **Business Card**, **Envelopes** and **Labels**.

4.  Return to the top of the display. Click the **A4 (Portrait)** option and click the **Create** button (or double click the option). A blank, single page publication is created, ready for editing.

A4 (Portrait)
21 x 29.7cm

5.  Notice the blue borders near the edge of the page. These are the page **Margins Guides** and are used to help with object alignment. They will be described in the next exercise.

6.  From the **Objects** toolbar, click the **Text Box** tool, ▣.

7.  Click and drag with the cursor to draw a box near the centre of the page. Use the **Rulers** or the information on the Status Bar to make it about **14cm** wide by **3cm** high.

8.  When a text box is selected, text can be entered. Type **The Grand Canyon**.

9.  The default text size is very small. Select **Format | AutoFit Text | Best Fit**.

10. Save the publication as **geography** and leave it open for the next exercise.

# Exercise 9 - Layout Guides

### *Knowledge:*

Layout Guides are lines on a publication page which help to line up objects, either as a visual aid or by using the **Snap** option so that objects will 'stick' to guide lines as they are moved about. Because they appear on every page of a publication, they can help to maintain consistency between pages. **Layout Guides** are not printed.

**Margin Guides** define a nominal border around the page, **Grid Guides** divide the page into rows and columns, and **Ruler Guides** can be drawn in any position.

### *Activity:*

1.    In the **geography** publication, select **Arrange | Layout Guides** to display the **Layout Guides** dialog box.

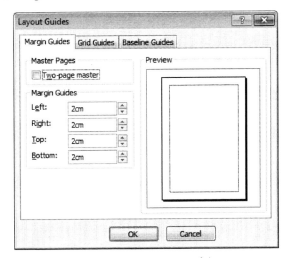

2.    Change all the **Margin Guides** to **3cm** and click **OK**.

3.    Guides can be added to divide the page into areas. Select **Arrange | Layout Guides** again and select the **Grid Guides** tab in the dialog box.

4.    Change the number of **Columns** to **3** and the number of **Rows** to **2**.

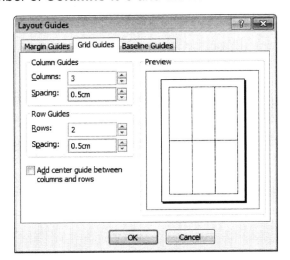

# Exercise 9 - Continued

5.  Click **OK**. Each grid line is shown as a double line because **Spacing** was specified between the guides. Notice that the spacing effects were not shown on the preview.

6.  Select **Arrange | Ruler Guides** and **Add Horizontal Ruler Guide**. A green horizontal guide line is added to the page.

7.  These can be moved up and down the page, and are useful for lining up objects. Click on the **Ruler Guide** and drag it up to be **5cm** from the top of the page. Use the **Rulers** or the **Status Bar** data to determine the position.

> **Note:**   The **Ruler Guides** *dialog box (select* **Arrange | Ruler Guides | Format Ruler Guides***) allows the position of the ruler to be changed or more lines to be added.*

8.  Select **Arrange | Snap**. Make sure the option **To Guides** is checked so that when an object is being moved around a page, it will tend to 'snap' to the guides when close to them. Click on the page if the option is already checked.

9.  Select the text box and make sure **Zoom** is set to **100%**. Move the text box slowly up towards the **Ruler Guide** and left towards the left **Margin Guide**. As the box approaches the guides, notice how it tends to jump and stick to the guides. This is a subtle effect but can be very useful to ensure accurate consistent positioning.

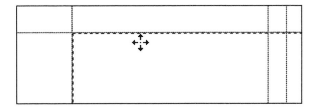

10. Draw another text box exactly fitting the two lower right panels on the page, formed by the layout guides and the margin guides, as indicated below.

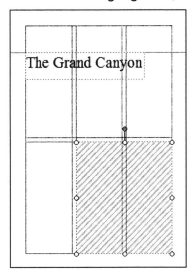

11. Save the publication and leave it open for the next exercise.

# Exercise 10 - Importing Text Files

### Knowledge:

Instead of typing text into text boxes, existing text files can be inserted. This is useful if large quantities of required text already exist in a different application. It also means that text entry and formatting can be done in a more specialised application such as *Microsoft Word*, and the results imported into *Publisher*.

### Activity:

1.  Make sure the lower text box in the **geography** publication is selected and click **Insert | Text File** to display the **Insert Text** dialog box.

2.  In the dialog box, locate the supplied data folder for this unit, (see exercise 4 for more information), and make sure that **All Text Formats** is selected in the **File types** drop-down list.

3.  Select the **Holiday** file. This is a **Word Document** file (.**docx**). This file type supports all the varied formatting options available within *Word*.

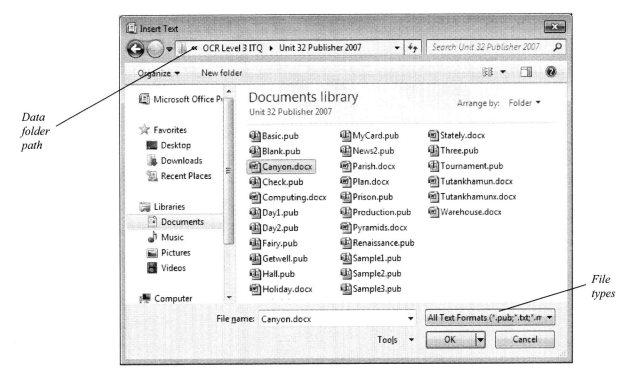

4.  Click **OK**. There will be a message displayed as the file is converted for use within *Publisher* and then the file is inserted into the text box. This may happen whenever a text file is inserted. Notice that the formatting from the original file is maintained.

> **Note:**  *Be aware that any features that are not supported by Publisher – **Footnotes** for example –, will not be imported.*

5.  This is not the correct file for this publication. Leave the publication open for the next exercise where it will be corrected.

# Exercise 11 - Text Overflow

### *Knowledge:*

Sometimes when inserting text files into text boxes, there will not be enough room for it all and a text overflow will occur. *Publisher* can deal with this by applying **Autoflow**, where text flows automatically to another text box. If another text box is not available, *Publisher* can create one.

### *Activity:*

1.    Make sure the lower text box in the **geography** publication is selected and press <**Ctrl A**> to select all of the text.

2.    Select **Edit | Delete Text** or press the <**Delete**> key to remove the text.

3.    Insert the **Canyon** text file as before.

4.    A **Text in Overflow** button, **A···**, will be displayed at the bottom of the box, showing that not all of the available text will fit in the box and some is not displayed. A message is displayed asking if you want to use **autoflow**.

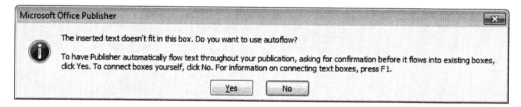

5.    Read the message and click **Yes**.

6.    There are no other available boxes so a message asks if you *Publisher* is to create them. Read the message and click **Yes**.

7.    A message is displayed confirming that *Publisher* has created a new text box on a new page. Click **OK**.

8.    A new page 2 is displayed. *Publisher* has created a text box the size of the page to contain the overflow text. Drag the top left corner of the text box until the box fits the same lower right area as the box on page 1.

9.    The two text boxes are now **Linked**. Click **Go to Previous Text Box** ⬅🔲 above the box on page **2**. The linked text box on page 1 is displayed.

10.   Save the modified publication and close it.

# Exercise 12 - Linked Text Boxes

### Knowledge:

Text boxes can be linked before any text is added. This means that when text is added the flow of text between the boxes is automatic. Any number of boxes can be linked.

### Activity:

1. Open the publication **Blank**. This contains three empty text boxes, arranged side by side in the upper part of the page.

2. Click in the first (left) text box and click **Create Text Box Link**, from the **Connect Text Boxes** toolbar.

3. Move the cursor over the next (centre) left text box where it becomes a pouring jug, , and click once. This box is now linked to the first one, even though there is no text present.

4. Click **Create Text Box Link** again and click in the next (right) text box. The three text boxes are now dynamically linked. Select the centre box. It shows links to a **Previous** and a **Next** box.

5. Select the left text box. Select **Insert | Text File** and insert the file **Canyon**. After conversion, the file is inserted automatically across all three boxes.

6. The link is dynamic. Select the left text box and click in front of the title text, **Geography of the Grand Canyon**. Press <**Enter**> twice to add two blank lines. The text flow between the boxes is changed to accommodate this.

7. Select the centre text box and drag it down to the lower central cell formed by the layout guides. The text flow is unaffected.

8. With the centre text box selected, select **Break Forward Link**, , from the **Connect Text Boxes** toolbar. The third text box is no longer linked and now there is text overflow which is not displayed.

9. The text is not lost. Click **Create Text Box Link** again and click in the right text box. The extra text is displayed again.

10. Save the publication as **linked boxes** and close it.

# Exercise 13 - Alternative Text Entry

### Knowledge:

Typing text in using a keyboard is probably the most common form of data entry at this level, but it is not the only method. There are other input methods which can be used, for example:

| | |
|---|---|
| **Scanner** | Existing documents can be scanned and the content copied into the publication. |
| **Voice Recognition** | There are systems which will convert audio information (voice) into text which can be added to the publication. |
| **Touch Screen** | Allows selections to be made from a list of displayed options. |
| **Stylus** | Allows text to be 'written' on a special tablet and converted into digital information which can be added to the publication. |
| **Copy** | Text and images can be copied from any source available to your computer, e.g. documents, messages or web pages, and pasted into the publication. |

When using any content that is copied or imported from a different source, you need to be very aware of **Copyright** constraints. The effect of copyright on the day to day use of IT is that any text or picture scanned in – any graphic image, audio or video file downloaded or copied from the Internet or from any other source – cannot be used in a publication, unless specifically identified by its owner as being copyright-free. Content may be used if the owner has given explicit consent, but then it is usual to include a reference to acknowledge the source of the material.

Entering text which is a copy of someone else's work or ideas, and passing it off as your own, is **Plagiarism**. This is not necessarily illegal, but it is usually considered as immoral. If you are quoting from someone's work, a reference must be given.

If any personal data referring to any identifiable individuals is used, you must be fully aware of the implications of the current **Data Protection Act**. Amongst other things, this legislation states that any such information must be:

- Obtained and processed fairly and lawfully

- Processed only for one or more specified and lawful purposes

- Adequate, relevant and not excessive for those purposes

- Accurate and kept up-to-date

- Kept for the original purpose only and for no longer than is necessary

- Processed in line with the rights of the individual

If any such data is to be used, make sure you have considered the implications of the complete act. It is advisable not to include any personal information on others, for instance employees or club members, in a publication unless the act has been fully considered.

### Activity:

1.  Create a blank **A4 Portrait** publication. Draw a text box to fill the upper half of the page, and another to fill the lower half.

2.  In the upper box, insert the text file **Pyramids**.

3.  Use click and drag to highlight the first paragraph in the text (increasing the zoom to 100% will help).

4.  Select **Edit | Copy** or click the **Copy** button 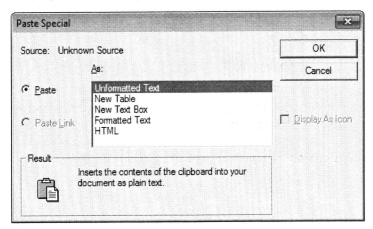 on the **Standard** toolbar.

5.  Click in the lower text box and select **Edit | Paste** or click the **Paste** button on the **Standard** toolbar. The text is copied into the new box.

6.  At the end of the pasted text, press **<Enter>** to create a new line.

| | |
|---|---|
| **Note:** | *This copy and paste process can be used to copy text (or images) from any other source, e.g. from another publication, document, web page.* |

7.  Without closing *Publisher*, start your browser application and display the web site **www.bigplanetsupport.co.uk**.

8.  Use click and drag to select any paragraph of text.

9.  Right click on the selected text and select **Copy** from the shortcut menu.

10. Close your browser application and make sure the *Publisher* window is displayed.

11. Click in the new text box below the inserted line and select **Edit | Paste Special** to display the **Paste Special** dialog box.

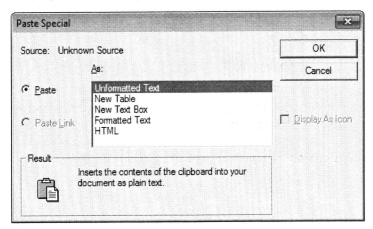

12. It is necessary to lose all of the web page formatting that might be associated with this text. Make sure **Unformatted Text** is selected and click **OK**.

| | |
|---|---|
| **Note:** | *The text from the web page is pasted into the text box. Notice that any text formatting such as fonts and effects will also be lost.* |

13. Close the publication <u>without</u> saving.

# Exercise 14 - Editing Text

## Knowledge:

It is often necessary to change text after it has been entered, because of errors or alterations. Text can be easily inserted, amended or deleted. For anyone familiar with word processing applications such as *Microsoft Word,* it is worth remembering that many of the editing (and formatting) techniques used there are also available in *Publisher.* As in *Word*, text must be selected before editing.

## Activity:

1.   Publications can be created directly from *Word* documents. From the **Getting Started** screen, with no publications open, select **File | Import Word Document**.

2.   Locate supplied data folder in the **Import Word Document** dialog box and double click on the **Plan** document. A new publication is created with a single text box filling the page margins which contains the **Plan** document text. Set a **Zoom** of **Page Width**.

3.   Text is entered where the cursor is flashing (the **Insertion Point**). Click in the first line of text then press the <**Home**> key to move to the start of the line.

4.   Type **Planning Terms** and press <**Enter**>.

5.   In paragraph 5, click and drag to highlight the text **and VDUs**. Press the <**Delete**> key once to delete the text.

6.   Click the **Undo** button ⤺ on the **Standard** toolbar. The entry is reversed and the original text is back. Click **Redo**, ⤻, to delete the word again.

7.   In paragraph 6, click and drag to highlight the text **VDUs**. Type **terminals** to replace the text.

8.   Click the **Special Characters** button, ¶, on the standard toolbar. This will display all special non-printing characters in the text, particularly the **Paragraph** mark, ¶.

9.   Use click and drag to highlight all of paragraph **6** including the header and the paragraph mark at the end.

10.  Click the **Cut** button, ✂, on the toolbar (or select **Edit | Cut**).

11.  Click at the end of the last paragraph and press <**Enter**>.

12.  Click the **Paste** button, 📋, on the toolbar (or select **Edit | Paste**). The paragraph has been relocated.

13.  Use click and drag to highlight all of paragraph **4** including the header and the paragraph mark at the end.

# Exercise 14 - Continued

14. Click anywhere in the highlighted text and drag the insertion mark down to the blank line at the end of the text. Release the mouse button to relocate the text.

15. Change the paragraph numbers (by overtyping) to reflect the new order.

16. Click at the beginning of the title on the first line and select **Edit | Replace**. The **Find and Replace** task pane is displayed.

17. Enter **work** in **Find what** and **job** in **Replace with**.

18. Click **Find Next**. The first use of **work** in the text is highlighted.

19. Click **Replace** to replace it with **job**. The next example of **work** is found.

20. This is not suitable for changing so click **Find Next**. Click **Replace** when the next example is found.

21. Keep pressing **Replace** until a message is displayed to say that the search is finished. Click **OK**.

22. It is possible to change <u>all</u> occurrences of a word with a different word in a single step. In the **Find and Replace** task pane, enter **job** in **Find what** and **work** in **Replace with**. Click **Replace All**.

23. All examples of **job** are automatically replaced with **work**. Click **OK** at the message.

24. Save the publication as **example** in the supplied data folder.

25. Any text may be edited (and formatted) in *Microsoft Word*. With the text box selected, select **Edit | Edit Story in Microsoft Word**. Your copy of *Word* will be started and the text from the text box will be displayed as a document. Notice the **Title Bar**. This is the **example** publication which is being edited, <u>not</u> the original **Plan** document.

26. Highlight all of paragraph **3** and delete it.

27. Click the **Office Button** in the top left of the *Word* window and select **Close & Return to example** to return to *Publisher* with the text amended.

> **Note:** *If the text is not displayed properly on return, change the **Zoom** setting to refresh the view.*

28. Close the publication <u>without</u> saving.

# Exercise 15 - Develop Your Skills

You will find a *Develop Your Skills* exercise at the end of each Skill Set. Work through it to ensure you've understood the previous exercises.

1.  Create a blank **A4 Portrait** publication.

2.  Draw a text box **10cm** high to fit in the top of the page margins.

3.  Insert the text file **Stately**. Do <u>not</u> let *Publisher* create any extra text boxes to deal with the overflow.

4.  Draw another identical text box to fit in the lower part of the page between the page margins.

5.  Link the upper text box with the lower text box so that the missing text is fully displayed.

6.  Draw a text box **2cm** high and **6cm** wide, between the existing text boxes.

7.  Use cut and paste to move the **Toffington Hall** heading from the text to the central text box.

8.  Add a blank line before each of the subheadings (**The House**, **The Gardens**, etc.).

9.  Delete the last two lines in the **Garden** item (concerning the maze).

10. Change the **Tea Room** opening times to **10.00am to 5.00pm**.

11. Save the publication as **skills2** and close it.

12. Create another blank **A4 Portrait** publication.

13. Draw a **10cm** by **10cm** text box near the centre of the page.

14. Select **File | Import Word Document**.

15. Select the file **Holiday** from the supplied data and click **OK**. What happens?

16. Close all open publications <u>without</u> any further saving.

# Summary: Creating Publications

In this Skill Set you have seen some of the basic principles of creating a new publication. You have seen how to add text boxes and various methods of entering text into them. You have learnt some of the consequences of using information from other sources, particularly the implications of copyright law and data protection act.

You have also seen how text may be flowed between several different text boxes.

<u>Your OCR ITQ evidence must demonstrate your ability to:</u>

- Input information into publications from a variety of sources, including importing information produced using other software

- Identify copyright constraints, including:
  - Copyright law
  - Acknowledgements
  - Plagiarism
  - Data Protection Act

- Select and use appropriate editing and formatting techniques:
  - Control text flow between boxes

# Skill Set 3

# Text Formatting

By the end of this Skill Set you should be able to:

Use Simple Formatting

Use Styles

Use Schemes

Define Margins

Create Columns

# Exercise 16 - Simple Formatting

### Knowledge:

Any text in a text box can have a variety of formatting applied. Basic formatting can include setting Font (type and size), Colour, Alignment and Effects.

### Activity:

1.    Open the **Hall** publication. Make sure the text box is selected and zoom is set to **100%**.

2.    All text is currently in the default **Normal** style which for this page is **Times New Roman** font, **10 pt**. This is shown in the **Formatting** toolbar.

3.    Press <**Ctrl A**> to select all the text in the box.

4.    Click the drop down arrow of the **Font** box on the **Formatting** toolbar and select **Arial**. Select **11** in the **Size** box.

5.    Use click and drag to select the heading, **Toffington Hall**. Change the font size to **14pt** and click the **Bold** button on the **Formatting** toolbar, **B**, and, click the **Center** alignment button, ☰.

6.    Click the drop down arrow on the **Font Color** button, **A▾**, and select **More Colors** and select a dark blue colour from the **Standard** tab. Click **OK** to apply the colour. Click away to see the effect.

7.    Select the first two paragraphs of text and click the **Justify** alignment button, ☰.

8.    Select the second heading, **The House**. Format it as **12pt**, **Bold** and **Underlined**.

9.    Leave the heading selected and double click the **Format Painter** button, ⬰.

10.    Click and drag with the new cursor to highlight the next heading, **The Gardens**. The same formatting is applied.

11.    Highlight the headings **Pets' Corner**, **Gift Shop** and **Tea Room** in turn to apply the same formatting.

12.    Click the **Format Painter** button again (or press <**Esc**>) to cancel the feature.

13.    Save the publication as **hall2** and close it.

# Exercise 17 - Styles

**Knowledge:**

A text **Style** is a named collection of text effects including font, size, alignment, spacing, etc. Once created, it can be easily applied to text anywhere in your publication. All text with the same style will look the same, which helps to maintain consistency of appearance throughout a publication.

**Activity:**

1. Open the **Hall** publication, select the text box and zoom in to **100%**.

2. Select **Format | Styles** to display the **Styles** task pane.

| Note: | The **Styles** task pane can also be opened using the **Styles** button, on the toolbar. |
|---|---|

3. Move the cursor over the **Heading 1** style – a tooltip appears describing the style, including what style it is based on and which extra formatting is applied. It is based on the **Normal** style but is **16pt**, **Bold** and **Centred**. There is an extra **12pt** space after each paragraph (expressed as 0.423cm).

> Heading 1: Normal + 16pt, Bold, Center, Space after 0.423cm

4. Select the first heading (**Toffington Hall**) and click **Heading 1** from the task pane. The formatting of this style is applied (click away to see it).

5. Select the second heading (**The House**) and click **Heading 2** from the task pane. The formatting of this style is applied.

6. Apply the **Heading 2** style to the remaining headings on the page.

7. The benefits of styles can be shown by changing **Heading 2**. Move the cursor over the **Heading 2** style in the task pane, click the drop down arrow and select **Modify**.

8. Click **Font**. Click the **Underline** drop down arrow in the **Font** dialog box and select **Single**.

9. Click **OK**, then **OK** again. <u>All</u> instances of **Heading 2** styled text are changed.

# Exercise 17 - Continued

10.  New styles can also be created. Click **New Style** from the task pane to display the **New Style** dialog box.

11.  Enter the new style name as **Main Header** and click **Font** to display the **Font** dialog box. Choose **Arial Black**, **Italic**, **24pt**. Make the colour **Gold**.

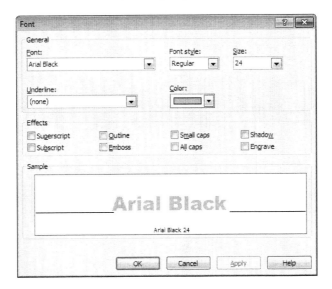

12.  Click **OK** to apply the formatting to the style.

13.  Use the **Paragraph** button to change the text **Alignment** to **Center**.

14.  Select the first heading again (**Toffington Hall**), and then click **Main Header** from the **Styles** task pane. The formatting of the new style is applied.

| **Note:** | *Applying* **Font Schemes** *automatically generates many new styles.* |
|---|---|

15.  Select **Format | Format Publication** to display the **Format Publication** task pane.

16.  Click **Font Schemes**, Aª **Font Schemes** .

17.  Click on **Apex** from the list of **Font Schemes**. The normal text style is changed to **Book Antiqua**, and all headings become **Lucida Sans Unicode**. Click in the text to verify this.

| **Note:** | *Don't worry if the text has overflowed the text box at this stage.* |
|---|---|

18.  Scroll down the list of **Font Schemes** and select **Deckle**. The normal text is changed to **Gill Sans MT**, and all headings become **Papyrus**.

19.  Font schemes also introduce a number of other styles, even if they are not actually used at present. Select **Format | Styles** to see the list of styles now available.

20.  Save the publication as **formatted** and leave it open for the next exercise.

# Exercise 18 - Text Box Formatting

### Knowledge:

A number of text formatting features can also be applied by formatting the **Text Box** itself.

### Activity:

1.  With the **formatted** publication open, make sure the text box is selected.

2.  Select **Format | Text Box** and select the **Text Box** tab.

3.  Set all the **Text Box Margins** to **0.3cm** and select **Best fit** from **Text autofitting**.

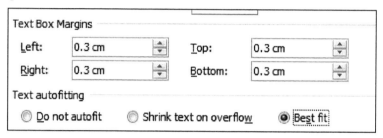

4.  Click **OK**. There is now space between the text box edge and the text, and all text is resized to fit the box.

5.  Select **Format | Text Box** and select the **Colors and Lines** tab.

6.  Click the **Color** drop down arrow in the **Fill** section and click **More colors**. Select very pale blue colour and click **OK**.

7.  Click the **Color** drop down arrow in the **Line** section and select a dark blue colour. Accept the default of a single line around the whole box.

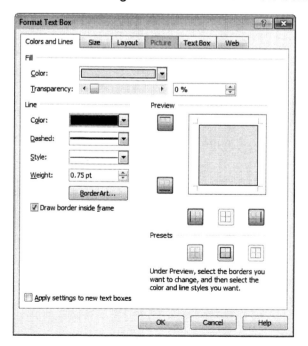

# Exercise 18 - Continued

8.     Look at the other options available when adding lines then click **OK**. The text box is now shaded pale blue with a dark blue border.

9.     Draw a new text box inside the top of the existing text box, between the margin guides and **2.5cm** high. Enter the text **Stately Homes of the North**.

10.     Format this text as **Papyrus** font, **28pt**, **bold** and **centred**. Shade the text box with a very pale pink colour and apply a default border of dark blue.

11.     Select **Format | Text Box** and select the **Text Box** tab. Use the drop down list to set the **Vertical alignment** to **Middle**.

12.     Click **OK**.

13.     With the top text box selected, select **Arrange | Rotate or Flip | Rotate Left 90**. The text box is rotated.

14.     Click and drag the text box to line up with the left margin guide, then extend the text box from the top to the bottom guide.

15.     Extend the main text box to the top margin guide.

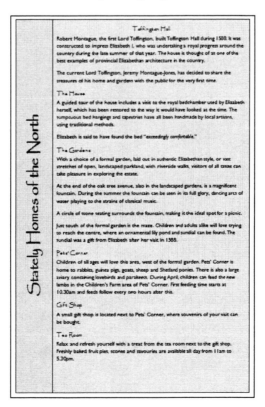

16.     Save the **formatted** publication and leave it open for the next exercise.

# Exercise 19 - Columns

### Knowledge:

Columns divide the text vertically into sections within a text box. This is a different way of presenting text, which can look really effective in certain publications (such as a newsletter, for example).

Organizing text into columns can be done before or after the text has been entered.

### Activity:

1.  The **formatted** publication should be open from the previous exercise. Make sure the main text box (the largest one) is selected then select **Format | Text Box** to display the **Format Text Box** dialog box.

2.  Select the **Text Box** tab. Notice that the **Columns** button is ghosted, i.e. not available. **Columns** and **Best fit** cannot be selected together.

3.  Select **Do not autofit** to switch off **Best fit**, then click the **Columns** button.

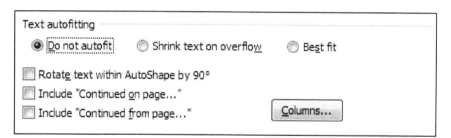

4.  In the **Columns** area, change the number of columns to **2** and the **Spacing** between the columns to **0.5cm**.

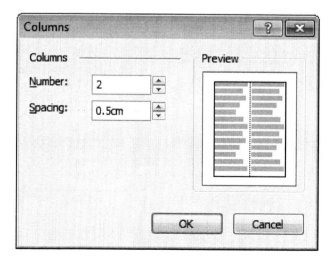

5.  Click **OK** and **OK** again to divide the box into two columns.

# Exercise 19 - Continued

6.  Save the **formatted** publication and close it.

7.  Open the **Three** publication. This shows the **Canyon** text document spread between three linked text boxes, as described in a previous exercise.

8.  Draw a text box filling the lower half of the screen and insert the **Canyon** text file. The text will overflow, but remember, it is not lost. Do <u>not</u> use Autoflow.

9.  Select **Format | Text Box** and select the **Text Box** tab and click **Columns**.

10. Set the number of columns to **3** with a spacing of **0.5cm** and click **OK**, then **OK** again.

---

**Note:**   *The single text box with columns produces a very similar looking result to the three linked text boxes in the upper half of the page. The linked text boxes, however, can be manipulated individually, and so this is generally accepted as the more flexible solution.*

---

11. If the columns of text in a box are unbalanced (different sizes) there are several ways to correct this. One way is to change the font or font size. Select all the text in the lower box and change the font to **Arial**. The columns are slightly better balanced.

12. Select **Undo**, [↶], to revert to the original font size.

13. Another way to balance columns is to change the box size. Drag the bottom edge of the text box upwards to reduce the size of the box. By trial and error find a size that displays all of the text (no text overflow) but gives a better balance. Reducing the height by about 1cm balances the columns but does not necessarily give the best looking result.

| contains·volcanic·debris,·old· lava·flows·and·igneous·rock.· The·northern·plateau,·the· | Climate. ¶ | many·of·the·rock·strata· forming·the·gorge·walls·are· composed·of·marine· sediment.·¤ |
|---|---|---|

14. Return the text box to its original size. Another option is to add extra content. Position the cursor immediately in front of the **Climate** heading and press <**Enter**> four times. This maintains the paragraphs better but doesn't look very good.

15. A picture or graphic could be inserted in the gap. This will be described in a later exercise. For this exercise click **Undo** to remove the blank lines.

16. It can be seen from these few steps that achieving optimum appearance for text in columns can be a time consuming operation. It is easier with linked boxes as the appearance of each box can be 'tuned' separately. Save the publication as **columns** and close it.

# Exercise 20 - Develop Your Skills

You will find a *Develop Your Skills* exercise at the end of each Skill Set. Work through it to ensure you've understood the previous exercises.

1.   Create a blank **A4 (Portrait)** publication and draw a text box to fill the page up to the page margins. Insert the text file **Parish** and apply **Best Fit** so that the text fills the box.

2.   Change the font of all text in the text box to **Bookman Old Style**.

3.   The text is made up of a series of seven short articles. Add a blank line after every article title.

4.   Format the text box to have 2 columns of text with a **0.5cm** space between.

5.   Format each article heading to be **14pt** and centred.

6.   Delete the text **of Praise** from the **Beltones** article heading.

7.   Add a new paragraph in the middle of the **Brass Band** article, with the text: **Local resident Winifred Devine, who used to sing with the Rhythm Twisters, will be appearing with the band**.

8.   There has been an embarrassing mistake. The name of the village has been misspelled. Use **Find and Replace** to replace the word **Stripling** with **Strippling** wherever it appears.

9.   Change <u>all</u> margins of the text box to **0.5cm**.

10.  Add blank lines before the **Brass Band** heading so that it appears in column 2.

11.  Highlight all of the text in the text box and apply a dark blue colour.

12.  Save the publication as **parish news** and close it.

13.  Open the **Renaissance** publication.

14.  Select the main title on page 1 and format it as **Forte 20pt** font, dark blue colour and **left** aligned.

15.  Click on the **Definition** heading and create a new **Style** called **Subtitle**.

16.  Format the style as **Tahoma**, **11pt**, dark blue with **Shadow** effect.

17.  Apply the **Subtitle** style to all headings on all pages.

18.  Format the text box on page **1** so that the text is aligned vertically in the middle of the box.

19.  Save the publication as **skills3** and close it.

# Summary: Text Formatting

In this Skill Set you have seen some of the principles of editing and formatting text content on a publisher page.

You have seen how to change text and how to format it. Formatting can be achieved by individually altering the appearance of text by changing font, size, alignment and colour, or by the design and application of styles and font schemes.

You will also have learnt how text formatting can be affected by changing text box properties.

<u>Your OCR ITQ evidence must demonstrate your ability to:</u>

- Identify what editing and formatting to use:

- Select and use appropriate techniques to edit publications and format text including
    - Find and Replace
    - Undo and Redo
    - Font Schemes
    - Font
    - Size
    - Colour
    - Alignment

- Control text flow within multiple columns

# Skill Set 4

# Pictures

By the end of this Skill Set you should be able to:

Use Image Files

Import Images from Devices

Use Clip Art

Use WordArt

Draw Shapes

Fill Shapes

Combine Shapes

Use Text Wrapping

Position and Size Objects

# Exercise 21 - Image Files

### Knowledge:

Pictures are common components of most publications. They can be inserted into a publication from a variety of sources, but most often they are inserted from files stored on your computer.

### Activity:

1.    Create a blank **A4 (Portrait)** publication.

2.    Select **Insert | Picture | From File**. The **Insert Picture** dialog box is displayed, showing all of the available image files in the selected folder.

> **Note:**    *If the selected folder is not the supplied data folder, navigate to it now.*

> **Note:**    *Notice that suitable image files can have a variety of file types such as **jpg**, **gif** and **png**.*

3.    Click once on the file named **Puffins** to select it then click **Insert**.

4.    The puffins image is inserted in the centre of the page. The image should be selected (surrounding handles) and the **Picture** toolbar should be displayed.

5.    Move the cursor over the picture. It changes to the move cursor.

6.    Click and drag to move the picture towards the lower left corner of the page.

7.    Click on the upper right corner handle and drag it outwards a little (about **2cm**) to increase the size of the image.

8.    Notice that whichever way the corner handle is dragged, the proportions of the image (height to width) always remains constant. Increase the picture height to about **10cm** (use the object dimensions on the **Status Bar**).

9.    Now click the centre handle of the right edge and drag it to the right page margin. The width changes but not the height, so that the image is distorted.

10.   With the picture selected, select **Arrange | Rotate or Flip**. Examine the options here, then select **Flip Horizontal**. The picture is flipped over.

11.   Select **Arrange | Rotate or Flip | Rotate Left 90⁰**. The picture turns.

12.   Locate the **Picture** toolbar and select **Reset Picture**, . The picture reverts to its original size as inserted. Rotating is also reversed.

# Exercise 21 - Continued

> **Note:**   *Positioning and flipping are not reversed. The top left corner position stays the same after reset.*

13. To add images another way, select the **Picture Frame** tool, [icon], from the **Objects** toolbar (not the **Picture** toolbar) and select **Empty Picture Frame**.

14. Draw a picture frame about **8cm** square in the upper part of the page and drag it to the top right corner of the page margins (move the puffin picture if necessary). The tooltip will identify this object as an **Empty Picture Frame**.

15. Right click on the frame and select **Change Picture | From File**. The **Insert Picture** dialog box is displayed.

16. Select **Puffins** and click **Insert**. The image is inserted within the frame, but maintains its proportions. This can be useful if picture frames are made part of a page design, acting as **placeholders** for images to be inserted later.

17. Click the **Crop** button, [icon], from the **Picture** toolbar. The handles around the image change.

18. Select the handle at the centre of the bottom edge and click and drag it up. Release the mouse button. The picture is cropped.

19. Crop the picture using the handles on the left, right and top of the picture to produce the following picture. Click away from the picture to remove the cropping handles.

20. Close the publication without saving.

# Exercise 22 - Importing Images from Devices

### Knowledge:

Publisher has the facility to import images directly from external devices such as cameras or scanners. However, you may find it is easier to simply download images from a device to a location on your computer, and then insert them into your publications in the usual way.

When devices with built in memory, such as digital cameras, are connected to your computer, they should appear as new devices within *Windows*. Images may then be inserted by navigating to the device and selecting the appropriate picture.

This exercise will give an example of how to copy images from a digital camera. If you have one, connect it now. If not, simply read this exercise for information.

### Activity:

1. Create a blank **A4 (Portrait)** publication.

2. Make sure your camera (with photos in memory) is connected to your computer and switched on.

> **Note:** *An **Autoplay** dialog box may be shown automatically when the device is connected. This would allow images to be downloaded onto your computer where they could then be imported as before. For this exercise, close the dialog box using the **Close** button.*

3. Select **Insert | Picture | From File**. In the **Insert Picture** dialog box, the camera is shown in the navigation pane as a **Removable Disk**.

4. Double click on this to display the content. You may have to navigate some folders to find the actual photos. In the example below, the path is:

**Computer / Removable Disk (F) / DCIM / 100PANA**

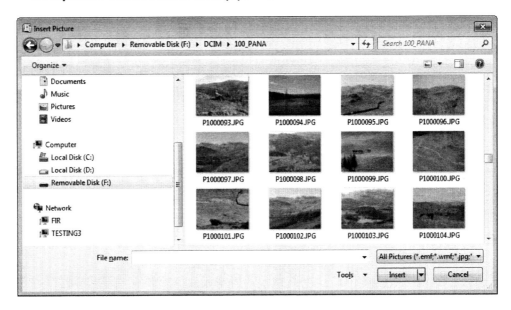

# Exercise 22 - Continued

5.  Select the required photograph and click **Insert**. The image is imported directly from the camera memory.

6.  Select **Insert | Picture | From Scanner or Camera** to display a dialog box.

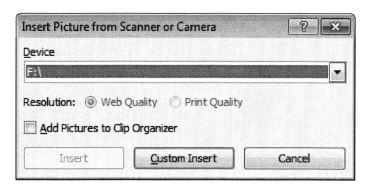

7.  Select the drive letter that corresponds to the connected device. In this example it is drive **F**.

8.  As the device is a camera with many images, it is necessary to select the required picture by clicking **Custom Insert**. The images on the device are found and presented for selection.

9.  Select the required image and click **Get Pictures** to import it.

> *Note:* *Alternatively, images may be imported using special device software. Different devices will have different downloading software, so you will need to know how to use the specific software for your particular device.*

10. Close the publication <u>without</u> saving.

> *Note:* *Selected pictures can be removed from a publication using the <**Delete**> key on your keyboard.*

# Exercise 23 - Clip Art

### Knowledge:

The **Clip Art** task pane is another source of images. These are sorted into categories, so the appropriate clip can be found quickly by searching. *Publisher 2007* automatically looks online for clips too, meaning you will have lots of choice.

### Activity:

1.    Create a blank **A4 (Portrait)** publication.

2.    Select **Insert | Picture | Clip Art**. The **Clip Art** task pane opens. Type in **rabbit** in the **Search for** box.

3.    Click the **Results should be** drop down arrow to see the file types that will be searched. Make sure **All media types** is selected and click away from the list.

4.    Click the **Go** button to see some graphics from this category.

| | |
|---|---|
| **Note:** | *The selection of pictures may vary depending on how your Publisher application has been installed.* |

5.    Click on the first picture in the panel. The picture is inserted on the page.

6.    Drag a corner handle of the picture to make the picture about **10cm** high. Move it up towards the top centre of the page.

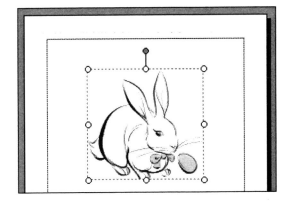

7.    Close the **Clip Art** task pane using the **Close** button.

8.    Save the publication as **hoppy** and leave it open.

# Exercise 24 - WordArt

### Knowledge:

**WordArt** is a feature that helps to create special text effects. It is ideally suited for use as a banner headline, which is a formatted title across the whole width of a page. A variety of different **WordArt** styles are available, such as stretched text, curved text, etc. It is best to apply the feature to small pieces of text only.

### Activity:

1.  Using the publication from the previous exercise, click in the lower part of the page and select **Insert | Picture | WordArt**. The **WordArt Gallery** is displayed.

2.  Select the example from the second column, fourth row and click **OK**. The **Edit WordArt Text** dialog box is shown.

3.  Type **Hoppy Birthday** and click **OK**. The text is inserted onto the page, and a **WordArt** toolbar is displayed.

4.  Move the cursor over the text. The tooltip indicates this is a WordArt object.

5.  Click and drag the object down to the lower part of the page.

6.  Drag a corner handle until the object is about **12cm** wide by **6cm** high. Centre the text.

> **Note:** Be careful – unlike **Pictures**, **WordArt** does <u>not</u> automatically maintain its proportion when enlarging.

7.  Save the publication and close it.

# Exercise 25 - Shapes

### Knowledge:

Simple drawn lines and shapes, known as **AutoShapes**, can easily be created within *Publisher*. These are available as an **Insert | Picture** option, or from the **Objects** toolbar.

### Activity:

1.    Create a blank **A4 (Portrait)** publication.

2.    Select the **Rectangle** drawing tool, ▢, from the **Objects** toolbar. In the lower left corner of the page, click and drag to draw a small rectangle.

| **Note:** | *Hold down <Shift> while drawing to create a perfect square.* |
|---|---|

3.    Use the **Oval** tool, ⬭, to draw an ellipse next to the rectangle.

| **Note:** | *Hold down <Shift> while drawing to create a perfect circle.* |
|---|---|

4.    Select the **AutoShapes** tool, 🔲, move the cursor slowly over each option to see the shapes available, then finally select **Basic Shapes**.

5.    From the pop up menu, select the lightning bolt, ⚡. Click and drag on the page to draw this shape.

6.    Select the **Line**, ╲ and click and drag on the page to draw a straight line.

7.    Click **AutoShapes** and select **Curve**, ⌐ from **Lines**. Click once on the page to anchor the start point of the line.

8.    Move the mouse down a little way and click again. Continue to do this until you have drawn a curved line, similar to the one in the diagram below.

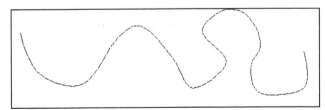

9.    Double click to finish the line.

10.    Click the drop down arrow on the **Line Color** button, 🖊, click **More Outline Colors** and select a dark green from the honeycomb.

11.    Try using other line drawing tools such as the **Freeform** tool, ▱, and the **Scribble** tool, ✎.

# Exercise 25 - Continued

12. Select any of the drawn lines, click the **Line/Border Style** button, 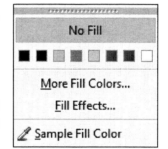, and select **3pt** from the list to make the line thicker.

13. Shading and other fill effects can be added to shapes. Select the lightning bolt shape on the page.

14. Click the drop down arrow on the **Fill Color** button, , on the **Formatting** toolbar.

15. Click the orange colour displayed to fill the shape.

16. Select the rectangle, click the **Fill Color** drop down and select **Fill Effects** to display the **Fill Effects** dialog box with the **Gradient** tab selected.

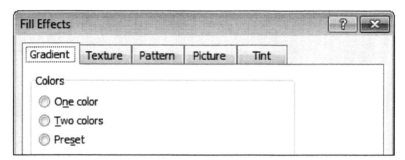

17. Select **Preset** from the **Colors** options and select **Daybreak** from the drop down list of **Preset colors**. Click **OK** to apply the effect.

18. Select the oval, display the **Fill Effects** dialog box and select the **Picture** tab.

19. Click **Select Picture** and make sure the contents of the supplied data folder are displayed in the dialog box. Select the **Dog** image and click **Insert**.

20. Text boxes may be shaded in exactly the same way. Draw a **6cm** by **2cm** text box and enter **Weather**. **Best Fit** the text to the box.

21. Display the **Fill Effects** dialog box and select the **Texture** tab. Select the second texture in the first column (**Water droplets**) and click **OK**.

22. Save the publication as **shapes** and then close it.

# Exercise 26 - Combining Shapes

### Knowledge:

Shapes and other objects can be combined to create more complex graphics. When objects overlap, it is important to specify their order in the 'stack', and when a composite picture has been created it can be grouped into a single object.

### Activity:

1.  Open the publication **Fairy**. This contains an **Oval** shape, a **Picture** (from **Clip Art**), and a text box.

2.  Move the crown picture to the middle of the oval shape. It cannot be seen because the oval is in front of it.

> **Note:** *The original order of objects depends on when they were added to the page.*

3.  Select the oval shape and select **Arrange | Order** to see the options. Select **Send to Back**. The oval is now behind the crown and the crown can be seen.

4.  Move the text box over the oval and arrange the objects in the following positions.

5.  To create a single object, all the individual components need to be selected. With the oval selected, hold down the **<Shift>** key and click on the crown, and then the text box. All shapes are now selected.

> **Note:** *Alternatively, draw a rectangle with the normal cursor, to surround all the shapes. Release the mouse button and all objects within the rectangle will be selected.*

6.  Select **Arrange | Group**. The three shapes are now grouped, that is they behave as if they were one object with one set of white handles.

7.  Click and drag the top left corner handle outwards a little. All shapes are resized and retain their relative positions.

8.  Drag the new object to a new location. All shapes move together as one.

9.  Select **Arrange | Ungroup**. The shape is three separate objects again.

10. Close the publication <u>without</u> saving.

# Exercise 27 - Text Wrapping

### Knowledge:

Text boxes and picture objects have usually been considered as separate objects in this guide up to now. It is common, however, for pictures to be included within text boxes and it is important to consider how the text and pictures will interact. Often, text will **wrap** around the picture.

### Activity:

1. On a blank publication, draw a text box that fills the whole page inside the margins. Insert the text file **Tutankhamun**.

2. With the text box selected, select **Insert | Picture | From File**.

3. Select the image file **Tut** from the supplied data and click **Insert**. Notice that all of the text is still visible. It automatically wraps around the picture.

4. Use click and drag to move the picture up so that it is in the centre of the text. Note how the text readjusts itself so that it always wraps around the picture.

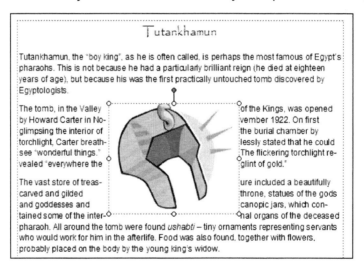

5. Click the **Text Wrapping** button, 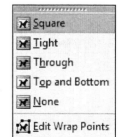, on the **Picture** toolbar to see the text wrapping options.

6. The default option is **Square**. The text can be made to wrap closer to the picture, but only if the background to the picture is transparent. Click the **Set Transparent Color** button, , on the **Picture** toolbar.

7. Click in a blank (white) area within the **Tut** picture borders.

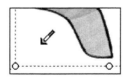

8. Click the **Text Wrapping** button and select **Tight** to see the effect.

# Exercise 27 - Continued

9.  Click the **Text Wrapping** button again and select **None** to switch off text wrapping. The picture is now on top of the text and some text is hidden.

10. Select **Arrange | Order | Send to Back**. The picture is sent behind the text and now all of the text can be seen over the picture (although not very well).

11. Select **Arrange | Order | Bring to Front**. The picture is put back on top.

12. Click the **Text Wrapping** button and select **Top and Bottom**. Text wrapping does not now extend to the sides of the picture, giving a more 'open' look.

13. Click the **Text Wrapping** button and select **Square** to apply the default wrapping again. Move the picture to the top left corner of the text box.

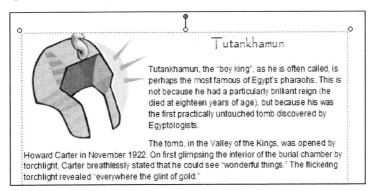

14. Save the publication as **king** and close it.

15. Open the **Production** publication. This has a text box with two columns with **1cm** spacing. The text in the columns is unbalanced.

16. Select **Insert | Picture | From File** and insert the picture **Factory**.

17. Select **Format | Picture** and select the **Size** tab in the dialog box. Set the **Width** to **7cm** and click **OK**.

18. Position the picture near the middle of the page. The default text wrapping is **Square** and text in both columns wraps around the picture.

19. Click the **Text Wrapping** button, 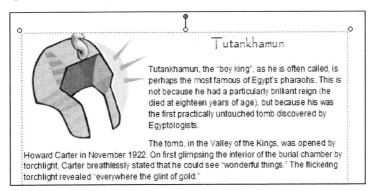, on the **Picture** toolbar and select **Top and Bottom**. Again, the text wrapping applies across both columns.

20. Move the picture so that it is completely inside the second column. Now the wrapping only applies to this column.

21. Adjust the picture position so that it is shown just above paragraph **7**. The text columns are now much better balanced.

22. Move the picture across to be completely inside the left column, just above paragraph **3**. This also produces a balanced effect. The exact size and position of any inserted picture can be adjusted to give the best result.

23. Close the publication <u>without</u> saving.

# Exercise 28 - Position and Size

### Knowledge:

All objects can be resized and moved quickly using the mouse to click and drag. There is, however, a more precise way of setting the position and size of objects.

### Activity:

1.  Create a blank **A4 (Portrait)** publication.

2.  Select **Insert | Picture | From File**. Locate the supplied data folder and select the **Puffins** file. Click **Insert**.

3.  Select **Format | Picture** to display the **Format Picture** dialog box.

| **Note:** | *Alternatively, right click the picture and select **Format Picture**.* |
|---|---|

4.  Select the **Layout** tab in the dialog box.

5.  In the **Position on page** section, change the **Horizontal** and **Vertical** values to **2cm**.

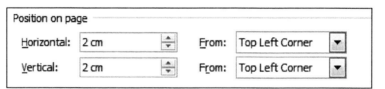

6.  Click **OK**. The picture is repositioned exactly.

7.  Select **Format | Picture** and select the **Size** tab in the dialog box.

8.  In the **Size and rotate** section, change the **Height** to **6cm**. Click in the **Width** box. This is automatically increased in proportion.

9.  Click **OK**. The picture is resized exactly.

10. Look at the **Status Bar** at the bottom of the screen. The exact position and size of the selected object is displayed.

| **Note:** | *All objects, including text boxes, can be formatted in exactly the same way.* |
|---|---|

11. Close the publication <u>without</u> saving.

# Exercise 29 - Develop Your Skills

You will find a *Develop Your Skills* exercise at the end of each Skill Set. Work through it to ensure you've understood the previous exercises.

1. Create a blank **A4 (Portrait)** publication. Insert the picture **Dog** from the supplied data.

2. Move the picture to the top half of the page and resize it to about **10cm** high, maintaining the proportions of the image.

3. Crop the image to focus on the dog's face, and centre the picture at the top of the page.

4. Deselect the image, and then insert a **Clip Art** picture at the bottom of the page. Search for **Cat** and insert any image that you like.

5. Enlarge the new image until is about **8cm** in height.

6. Insert **WordArt** between the pictures. Use any style and add text of **Animal News**. Resize the **WordArt** to about **6cm** in height.

7. Save the publication as **animal news** and close it.

> **Note:** *Check the sample publications in **Answers** at the end of the guide.*

8. Create a blank **A4 (Portrait)** publication. Draw a rectangle, an oval and a triangle from **Basic Shapes**.

9. Fill the triangle with any coloured gradient effect, fill the oval with the **Newsprint** texture, and fill the rectangle with the **Orchids** picture (use the **Picture** tab of the **Fill Effects** dialog box.

10. Arrange the shapes so that they look like this.

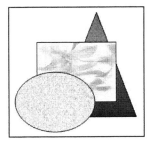

11. Group all the shapes so they become a single object.

12. Save the publication as **pictures** and close it.

# Exercise 29 - Continued

13. Open the **Prison** publication. This has two pages containing two linked text boxes.

14. On page **1**, insert the picture **Island**. Use **Format Picture** to set the picture width to exactly **12cm**, and its position to be exactly **2.0cm** in and **9cm** down from the top left corner of the page.

15. On page **2**, insert the picture **Hut**. Move it to the lower left corner of the margin guides.

16. Enlarge it so that it fits exactly between the margins (17cm wide), but stays aligned with the bottom margin guide.

17. Format the text box on page **2** to have **2** columns with the default spacing.

18. Insert the picture **Shark** into the text box. Move it into the first column and resize it so that it fits the column width as shown below. Use a button on the **Picture** toolbar to make the white picture background transparent.

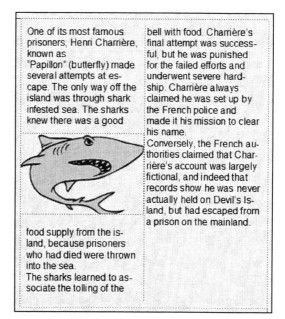

19. Select the **Shark** image and change the text wrapping to **None**. What happens to the text?

20. Change the text wrapping for the picture back to **Square**. Change the **Order** by selecting **Send to Back**. What happens to the text now?

21. Restore the original layout by selecting **Bring to Front**.

22. Remove the **Boundaries and Guides** from the view.

23. Save the publication as **island info** into the supplied data folder then close it.

# Summary: Pictures

In this Skill Set you have seen some of the basic principles of handling pictures in publications. You have seen how to insert pictures from stored image files or from external devices, and how to move, resize and crop them. You have also inserted pictures from the supplied Clip Art gallery

You have also seen how to draw and shade simple shapes and lines, and how to create pictures using WordArt. You have learnt how to combine pictures by grouping and how to control the order of objects which overlap.

Your OCR ITQ evidence must demonstrate your ability to:

- Organise and combine information of different types including:
    - Images
    - Text
    - Shapes
    - Text Wrapping

- Use graphic elements including:
    - Shapes
    - Lines
    - Shading
    - Grouping

- Manipulate images and graphic elements including:
    - Moving
    - Resizing
    - Maintain proportion
    - Cropping

# Skill Set 5

# Other Objects

By the end of this Skill Set you should be able to:

Use Tables

Insert Objects from Files

Link Objects

Hyperlinks

# Exercise 30 - Tables

### *Knowledge:*

Tables can be added to publication pages as a useful way to organise data. A table is just another object and can be manipulated like any other.

### *Activity:*

1.  Create a blank **A4 (Portrait)** publication. Click **Insert Table**, ⊞, from the **Objects** toolbar.

2.  Draw a rectangle about **8cm** wide by **5cm** high near the top of the page.

3.  The **Create Table** dialog box is displayed when you release the mouse button. Set **Number of rows** to **6**, **Number of columns** to **3**, and select **List 1** format.

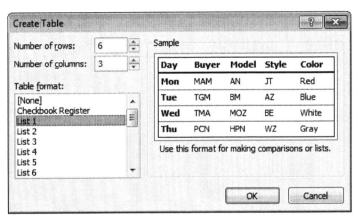

4.  Click **OK** to create the table. Next, enter data into the new table as shown below. Use <Tab> to move between cells. Use <F9> to zoom in if required.

| Day | Open | Close |
|---|---|---|
| Monday | closed | |
| Tuesday | 9:00 am | 5:00 pm |
| Wednesday | 9:00 am | 5:00 pm |
| Thursday | 9:00 am | 5:00 pm |
| Friday | 9:00 am | 8:00 pm |

5.  Select **Table | Select | Table** to select the whole table.

6.  Click the drop down arrow on the **Fill Color** button, 🎨▾, and select a light colour (so that the text is still clearly visible).

7.  Click and drag the table to the lower half of the page (hint: drag by the table border to move it).

8.  Save the publication as **opening times** and close it.

# Exercise 31 - Objects from Files

### Knowledge:

Objects can be created from existing files such as spreadsheets.

### Activity:

1. Create a blank **A4 (Portrait)** publication.

2. Select **Insert | Object** and select the **Create from file** option in the **Insert Object** dialog box.

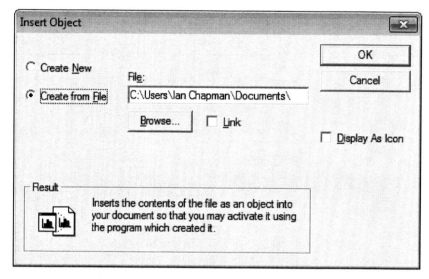

3. Click **Browse**.

4. Make sure the contents of the supplied data folder are displayed in the **Browse** dialog box. Select the **Sales** spreadsheet file and click **Open**.

5. Click **OK** in the **Insert Object** dialog box. Data from the workbook is inserted.

6. Drag the object to the top of the page and use the **Fill Color** button (**More Fill Colors**) to add a pale green background.

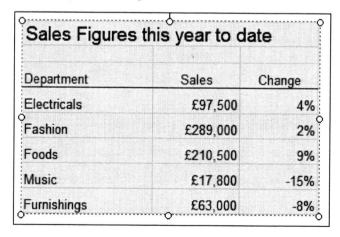

| Sales Figures this year to date | | |
| --- | --- | --- |
| Department | Sales | Change |
| Electricals | £97,500 | 4% |
| Fashion | £289,000 | 2% |
| Foods | £210,500 | 9% |
| Music | £17,800 | -15% |
| Furnishings | £63,000 | -8% |

7. Save the publication as **objects** and leave it open for the next exercise.

# Exercise 32 - Linked Objects

### Knowledge:

In the previous exercise, a copy of data held in a spreadsheet was **embedded** in a publication. It is possible, however, to insert an object which is **linked** back to the original source. Any changes in the original data will be shown in the publication.

### Activity:

1.  In the **objects** publication, make sure the existing object is <u>not</u> selected, and then select **Insert | Object**.

2.  Select the **Create from file** option and click **Browse**. Select the **Sales** spreadsheet again from the supplied data and click **Open**.

3.  This time select the **Link** option in the **Insert Object** dialog box.

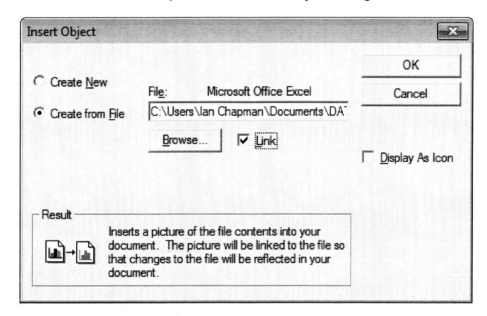

4.  Click **OK** to add the object. Position it just below the first table.

5.  Save the publication and close it.

6.  Start *Microsoft Excel* and open the **Sales** workbook. Click in cell **B4** and change the value to **98800**. Save the file and close it. Close *Excel*.

7.  In *Publisher*, open the **objects** publication. A message is displayed.

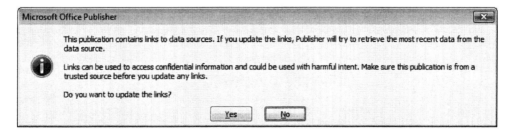

# Exercise 32 - Continued

8.  There is a choice of using the updated data or not. Click **Yes** to update the publication with the changed information. There may be a short delay as the data is updated.

9.  Look at the two data objects. The top, embedded object is unchanged. The lower, linked object reflects the latest version of the spreadsheet.

10. Select **Edit | Links**. Details of all linked files are listed in the **Links** dialog box.

11. Click on the one linked file that is displayed and review the options. Don't worry if there seems to be a display problem in this dialog box.

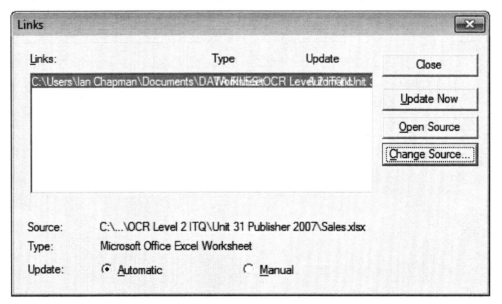

| Note: | **Update Now** will update the data from the current version of the source file. If **Manual** is selected from the **Update** options, this will be the only way to update the data. **Change Source** will allow a new source file to be selected. |

12. Click **Open Source**. The source file will be opened in the relevant application, in this case *Microsoft Excel*.

13. Close *Excel*.

14. Save the publication and close it.

# Exercise 33 - Hyperlinks

### Knowledge:

A **hyperlink** is a selection of text (or a picture) which, when clicked, takes the viewer of your publication to another location (within the same publication or to a page or file on the Internet). It can also link to an e-mail address.

### Activity:

1.  Select **Blank Page Sizes** from the *Publisher* **Getting Started** window.

2.  Scroll to the very bottom of window and select the first **Web Sites** blank page **(Web, 984x4608px).** Click **Create**.

3.  Insert the picture **Logo1** from the supplied data files.

4.  Draw a text box below the logo and enter the following text. The font size is **14pt**, it is **center** aligned and there is a blank line between each line of text.

5.  Highlight the text **web site** and select **Insert | Hyperlink**.

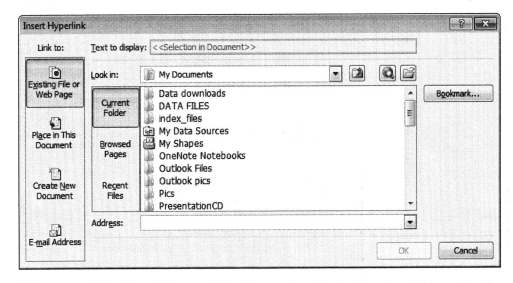

6.  Make sure **Existing File or Web Page** is selected on the left and in the **Address** box type **www.bigplanetsupport.co.uk**.

# Exercise 33 - Continued

7.  Click **OK**. Notice the selected text has changed colour, indicating that it is a hyperlink.

8.  Highlight the text **e-mail** and select **Insert | Hyperlink**.

9.  Make sure **E-mail Address** is selected on the left. In the **E-mail address** box type **trainer@bigplanetsupport.co.uk** and in the **Subject** box type **OCR ITQ**.

10. Click **OK**. The text changes colour, indicating it is another hyperlink.

11. Select **File | Web Page Preview**. The new publication is shown in your default web browser application.

12. Move the cursor over the **web site** text. The cursor changes to a pointing hand to indicate the presence of a hyperlink.

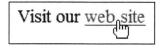

13. Click to open the home page of the *Big Planet Support* web site. Use the browser **Back** button to return to the publication.

14. Notice the link text is now a different colour, indicating that the link has been visited.

15. Click on **e-mail**. Your e-mail application will open showing a new e-mail addressed to *Big Planet Support*. A message could be added and the message sent, but for this exercise, close the e-mail application <u>without</u> saving.

| | |
|---|---|
| *Note:* | *There may be warning prompts before the application will open. If so, allow the website to run your e-mail program.* |

16. Close your browser application.

17. Hyperlinks can also be visited from within *Publisher*. Hold down the <**Ctrl**> key and move the cursor over the **web site** text on the publication page.

18. The pointing hand cursor is displayed. Click to open the web site as before.

19. Close your browser application.

20. Save the publication as **linkcheck** then close it.

# Exercise 34 - Develop Your Skills

You will find a *Develop Your Skills* exercise at the end of each Skill Set. Work through it to ensure you've understood the previous exercises.

| Regional Population | (millions) |
|---|---|
| 0 - 20 | 2.1 |
| 21 - 40 | 2.9 |
| 41 - 60 | 3.4 |
| over 60 | 2.4 |

1.    Create a blank **A4 (Portrait)** publication.

2.    Draw a table about **10cm** wide by **4cm** high in the top part of the page, and include the data shown on the right (use **List 4** style).

3.    Below this, insert an object created from the **Exports** spreadsheet file which can be found in the supplied data folder. Do <u>not</u> insert as a link.

4.    The inserted object is a pie chart and associated data table. Resize and reposition it to fit between the margins, and move it to the lower part of the page.

5.    Save the publication as **regional** and close it.

6.    Create another blank **A4 (Portrait)** publication.

7.    Insert an object created from the same **Exports** spreadsheet file as before, but this time, <u>do</u> insert it as a link. Resize the object to about **14cm** wide

8.    Save the publication as **regional linked** and close it.

9.    Start *Excel* and open the **Exports** spreadsheet.

10.   In the table, change the **Forestry** value (cell **C18**) to **6.4**. The chart changes automatically. Note the new **Forestry** percentage then save the spreadsheet and close it. Close *Excel*.

11.   Open the **regional** publication. What is the **Forestry** percentage?

12.   Open the **regional linked** publication. Click **Yes** at the update prompt. What is the **Forestry** percentage here?

13.   In the **regional linked** publication, draw a text box under the object and type **Data from norncensus.com**.

14.   Select the text, and insert a hyperlink to **www.bigplanetsupport.co.uk**. Use the <**Ctrl**> key to check that the link is working.

15.   Close the browser.

16.   Save the **regional linked** publication.

17.   Close all publications.

---

**Note:**   *Answers are listed in the **Answers** section at the end of the guide.*

# Summary: Other Objects

In this Skill Set you have seen how to include some of the other object types available to *Publisher*, including tables and objects created in other applications such as spreadsheets.

You will have learned how to embed external objects and how to include them so they are permanently linked to the original files.

You have also seen how to create and use hyperlinks to display external information.

Your OCR ITQ evidence must demonstrate your ability to:

- Include and reference information produced with other software, using:
    - Object Linking
    - Embedding
    - Hyperlinks

# Skill Set 6

# Multiple Page Layouts

By the end of this Skill Set you should be able to:

Manage Multiple Page Publications

Use Master Pages

Define Headers and Footers

# Exercise 35 - Multiple Pages

### Knowledge:

Publications can consist of more than one page. All of the features and formatting described previously can still be applied and some new features will be available.

### Activity:

1.    Create a blank **A4 (Portrait)** publication.

2.    Apply **Grid Guides** to divide the page into **2** columns and **2** rows.

3.    Draw a text box to fill the upper right area of the page (as defined by the grid guides).

4.    Select **Insert | Page**. Set the **Number of new pages** to **5** and select the **Duplicate all objects on page** option.

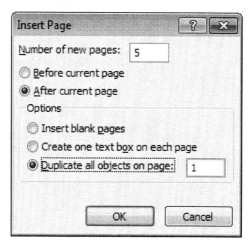

5.    Click **OK**. The publication now has six pages, as shown on the **Status Bar**.

6.    Click on the page **2** icon to display the second page. If a single page is shown, select **View | Two-Page Spread**. Pages **2** and **3** are shown together, as they would be seen if a book were opened.

7.    Click on the page **4** icon. All pairs of pages are now shown as two page spreads. Select **Edit | Delete Page**.

# Exercise 35 - Continued

8.     Leave **Both Pages** selected and click **OK**. Pages **4** and **5** are deleted.

9.     Select the first page and click in the text box. Imported text can be allowed to flow automatically into other existing text boxes if required.

10.     Select **Insert | Text File** and insert the supplied **Warehouse** document. The text will not fit the text box and a message is displayed.

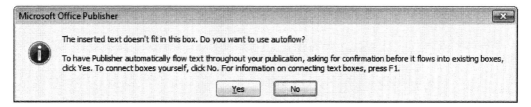

11.     Click **Yes**. The next available text box is selected and a new message is displayed (move the message if necessary to see the text box more clearly).

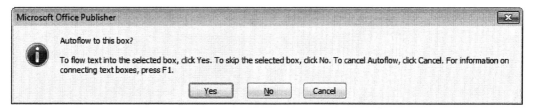

12.     Click **Yes**. The boxes are linked and text is inserted. There is still text left to be inserted so the third text box is selected and the message is repeated.

13.     Click **Yes** to link the text box on page **3**.

> **Note:** *The text boxes could have been linked manually either before or after the text file was imported.*

14.     Check each page to see how the text is spread over the three text boxes.

15.     View page **1**, select **Insert | Picture | From File** and insert the **Factory** picture. Move it to the centre of the text box.

16.     Look at page **3**. There is now more text in this text box.

17.     Save the publication as **multi** and close it.

# Exercise 36 - Master Pages

### Knowledge:

When a publication consists of more than one page and each page has common elements, such as the same background, headers, footers, logos, etc., then a **Master Page** can be used. This is a page which does not appear as part of the publication, but where all of the common objects for the publication are set out. Whatever appears on the **Master Page** appears automatically on every page of a publication (unless cancelled), and can only be amended in **Master Page** view.

Separate **Master Pages** can be defined for odd and even pages if required.

### Activity:

1.　Create a blank **A4 (Portrait)** publication.

2.　Click **View | Master Page**. The **Edit Master Pages** task pane is displayed and an **Edit Master Pages** toolbar. The screen background colour changes to remind you that this is the **Master Page**.

3.　Select **Format | Background** and click **More backgrounds** from the task pane.

4.　The **Fill Effects** dialog box is displayed. Select the **Picture** tab.

5.　Click **Select Picture** and navigate to the supplied data folder. Select the **Flower** file and click **Insert**. Click **OK** to add the picture as background.

6.　To define different odd and even page masters, click **Change Single-Page/Two-Page**, from the **Edit Master Pages** toolbar. Two master pages are displayed side by side. Make sure the **Zoom** is set to **Whole Page**.

7.　Click the **Layout Guides** button, from the toolbar to display the **Layout Guides** dialog box. Define **Grid Guides** to divide the page into **2** columns and **2** rows with no spacing and click **OK**. Grid guides are applied to both master pages.

8.　On the left master page, drag the vertical grid guide about **2cm** to the left. Notice that the guides on the right page mirror the effect.

9.　Select **Insert | Picture | From File** and insert the supplied **Factory** picture. Move the picture to the lower left corner of the left master page.

10.　Right click on the picture and select **Copy**. Right click on the right master page and select **Paste**. Move the picture to the lower right corner of the right master page.

# Exercise 36 - Continued

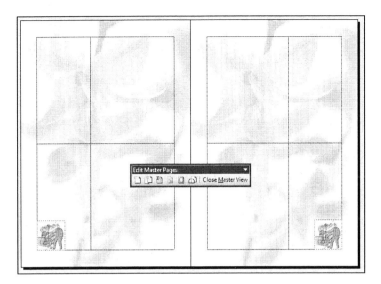

11.  Click **Close Master View** from the toolbar. The master view is closed and the first page of the publication is displayed again, ready for editing.

12.  Click the picture in the lower corner. The picture cannot be selected. A message will inform you that it is part of the **Master Page**.

13.  Draw a text box to fill the upper left area of the page (as defined by the grid guides). Format it to have a purple border with default settings.

14.  Select **Insert | Page**. Leave the **Number of new pages** as **1** and select the **Insert blank pages** option. Click **OK**.

15.  Look at page **2** (which is automatically selected). The background, grid guides and picture are all included on the new page because they are on the **Master Page**.

> **Note:**   *The text box is not included. To include it, you need to duplicate pages from existing ones.*

16.  Click **Undo** to reverse the page insert.

17.  Select **Insert | Page**. Increase the **Number of new pages** to **3**. This time select the **Duplicate all objects on page** option.

18.  Click **OK**. Now the text box is included on all of the new pages.

19.  On pages **2** and **4**, move the text box to the right to fit correctly.

20.  Select **View | Ignore Master Page**. All formatting from the master page is removed. Select **View | Ignore Master Page** again to replace it.

21.  Click in the text box on page **1** and insert the file **Computing** from the supplied data. Click **Yes** to all prompts concerning **Autoflow**.

22.  Save the publication as **multi2** and leave it open for the next exercise.

# Exercise 37 - Headers and Footers

### *Knowledge:*

Headers and Footers are text areas which appear at the top and bottom of every page in a publication. They can contain fixed items of text such as publication title or author name, or fields such as the date and time, and the page number, which can be added to a publication and set to automatically update.

The date and time can be entered as a fixed value, or can be set to automatically update every time the publication is opened or printed, to show the current date and time.

Headers and footers are created on the master page in a publication.

### *Activity:*

1.  The **multi2** publication should be open from the previous exercise. Display page **1** and select **View | Header and Footer**.

2.  **Master Page** view is automatically displayed. New text boxes have been added above and below the page margins for each Master Page. A small toolbar also appears.

3.  In the header text box for the left master, type **Computing**, then press <**Tab**> twice to move the cursor to the right end of the box, then type your name.

4.  Highlight all the text in the **Header**, increase the font size to **18pt**, and apply an **Italic** effect.

5.  In the header text box for the right master, type your name, then press <**Tab**> twice and type **Computing**. Format as **18pt, Italic**.

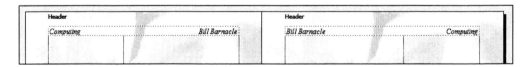

6.  Move to the **Footer** by clicking the **Show Header/Footer** button, :

7.  In the footer for the left master page, press the <**Tab**> key to move to the central position. Type **Page** followed by a space.

8.  Click the **Insert Page Number** button, , on the **Header and Footer** toolbar to insert the page number. A **#** symbol appears after **Page** (this is where the page numbers will appear in the publication).

# Exercise 37 - Continued

9. Press **<Tab>**. Select **Insert | Date and Time** to display the **Date and Time** dialog box.

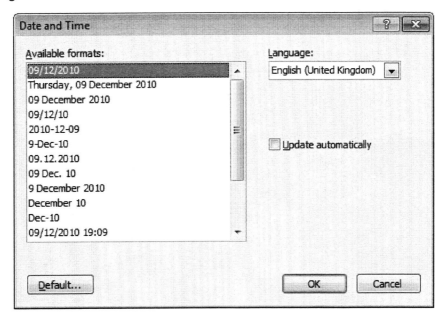

10. Select the format **dd/mm/yy**. To make sure the date is updated every time the publication is opened, place a check in **Update automatically**. Click **OK**.

11. Click in the footer for the right master page and enter the same date and page number fields, but this time insert the date on the left, press **<Tab>**, then insert the page number in the centre. Use the same format as before for both fields.

12. Click **Close** on the **Header and Footer** toolbar to return to the publication (or select **View | Master Page**). Make sure **Two-Page Spread** is selected and Zoom is set to Whole Page.

13. Examine each page to ensure the header and footer are on every page and alternate between different layouts for odd and even pages.

14. Display page **4** and select **Insert | Page**. Set the **Number of new pages** to **3** and select the **Insert blank pages** option.

15. Click **OK**. The new pages are added with all formatting from the **Master Pages**, including the appropriate header and footer information.

16. Save the **multi2** publication and close it.

# Exercise 38 - Develop Your Skills

You will find a *Develop Your Skills* exercise at the end of each Skill Set. Work through it to ensure you've understood the previous exercises.

1. Create a blank **A4 (Portrait)** publication. Select **Master Page** view.

2. Apply **Grid Guides** so as to define **2** rows, with no spacing.

3. Apply a vertical **Ruler Guide** positioned **8cm** from the left edge of the page.

4. Select **Format | Background** and select a **Texture Fill** of **Canvas**.

5. Draw a text box in the lower right part of the publication page, bounded by the **Margin Guides**, the horizontal **Grid Guide** and the vertical **Ruler Guide**.

6. Format the text box to have a red default border.

7. Insert five more pages after page **1**, duplicating the content of page **1**.

8. Switch to **Two-Page Spread** view. On all even pages, move the text box to line up with the left side margin guide.

9. Insert the text file **Computing** to the text box on page **2**. Answer **Yes** to all **AutoFlow** prompts.

10. Add the text **Computers** to the text box on page **1**. Apply **Best Fit** and centre the text vertically.

11. Use a field to add page numbers to the centre of the footer for all pages.

12. Use a field to add the date (automatically updating) to the page headers so that it appears on the left of odd pages and the right of even pages.

13. Add your name to the page headers so that it appears on the right of odd pages and the left of even pages.

14. In **Master View**, insert the picture **Logo1** in the top right corner of the margin guides on the left master, and the top left corner on the right master.

15. Save the publication as **skills6** and close it.

---

**Note:**    The first 3 pages of this solution are shown in the **Answers** section at the end of the guide.

---

# Summary: Multiple Page Layouts

In this Skill Set you have seen some of the special techniques which can be applied to multiple page documents.

You have seen how to use Master Pages to achieve a consistent appearance over any number of pages and how to add text and fields to page headers and footers.

Your OCR ITQ evidence must demonstrate your ability to:

- Control text flow:
    - Between pages

# Skill Set 7

# Web Publications

By the end of this Skill Set you should be able to:

Create a Web Publication

Create Navigation Links

Use Web Hyperlinks

Use Animations

Use Sounds

Use Web Page Preview

Save as a Web Page

Use Web Site Templates

# Exercise 39 - Creating Web Pages

### Knowledge:

Creating a web page publication from scratch is much the same as creating a print publication. Many of the formatting options and techniques will be the same, so this exercise will be something of a revision, although there will be some differences to notice. Some new types of object will be available.

### Activity:

1.  Make sure the **Getting Started** *Publisher* window is displayed and select **Web Sites**.

2.  Scroll down the main display to find **Blank Sizes**. Select **Web 984 x 4608px** and click **Create**. A blank publication is created. The **Title Bar** shows it as a **Web Publication**.

3.  Set the **Zoom** to **Page Width** then select **View | Toolbars** and make sure the **Web Tools** toolbar is selected.

4.  Select **Arrange | Layout** guides and use **Grid Guides** to define **2** columns with a spacing of **0px**. This will indicate the horizontal centre line for the page. Click **OK**.

5.  Draw a text box at the top of the page, across the entire width and **120px** high.

6.  Enter the text **Welcome to Egypt!**, centre it and apply **Best Fit**. Format the text to be very dark red.

7.  Select **Format | Background** to display the **Background** task pane. Click the background **Texture fill (Parchment)** from **More colors** to apply it.

| Note: | The background could have been applied to the **Master Page** then it would automatically appear on every page. |
|---|---|

8.  Select the text in the text box and change the font to **Georgia**.

| Note: | For Web publications, there are many fewer **Font** options available. |
|---|---|

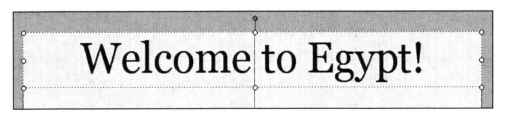

9.  Select **Insert | Page**. In the **Insert Page** dialog box choose to add **3** new pages, **After current page**, selecting the option to **Duplicate all objects on page 1**. Click **OK**.

# Exercise 39 - Continued

10. Change the heading text on page **2** to **Tutankhamun**, on page **3** to **The Pyramids**, and on page **4** to **The Nile**.

11. Return to page **1** and insert the picture **Egypt Map** from the supplied data, below the text box.

12. Select **Format Picture** from the **Picture** toolbar. On the **Size** tab, format the picture to be **530px** wide (ensure that **Lock aspect ratio** is checked). On the **Layout** tab set the position to be **230px** horizontal and **230px** vertical.

> **Note:**  *For Web publications, there are no **Text Wrapping** options available.*

13. Move to page **2** and insert the picture **Deathmask**. Set the width as **230px** and the position to be **380px** horizontal and **130px** vertical.

14. Draw a text box directly below the picture. Make it the full page width and **600px** high.

15. Insert the text file **Tutankhamun** into the text box. Apply **Best Fit**.

16. Format the text box to have **15px** margins on all sides.

17. Move to page **3** and insert the picture **Sunset**. Set the width as **300px** and the position to be **340px** horizontal and **130px** vertical.

18. Draw a text box directly below the picture. Make it the full page width and **340px** high.

19. Insert the text file **Pyramids** into the text box. Apply **Best Fit**.

20. Format the text box to have **15px** margins on all sides.

21. Save the publication as **egypt** and leave it open.

# Exercise 40 - Navigation Links

### Knowledge:

Although it is easy to change pages when viewing a publication in *Publisher*, when viewing as a Web publication in a browser, links are necessary to access all pages. Hyperlinks to each page could be added manually, but *Publisher 2007* includes a new object for Web publications called the **Navigation Bar** which helps to automate the process.

### Activity:

1.  Display page **1** of the **egypt** publication and select **Insert | Navigation Bar | New**.

2.  Various designs are listed. Select **Enclosed Arrow**. Look at the options on the right but do not change any.

3.  Click **Insert Object**. A new text box is added to the page. Drag it to the left, directly below the heading text box.

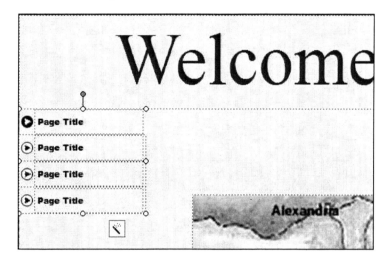

4.  Click the **Magic Wand** icon below the **Navigation Bar** to display the **Navigation Bar** properties dialog box.

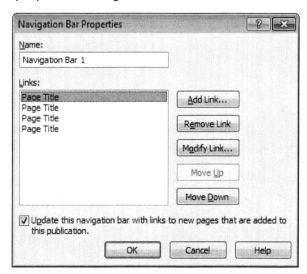

# Exercise 40 - Continued

5.    Links to all other pages have automatically been created but the displayed text can be easily changed. With the first page link selected, click **Modify Link**. The dialog box confirms that this link is to **Page 1** of this document.

6.    In **Text to display**, overwrite the existing text with **Home** then click **OK**.

7.    In the same way, change the **Text to display** for all the other links as follows:

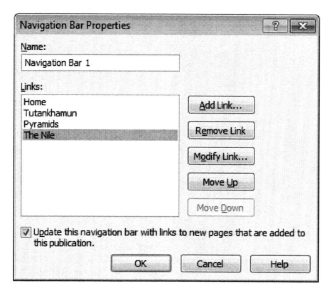

8.    Click **OK**. The **Navigation Bar** is changed.

9.    The links can be tested without using the browser. Hold down the <**Ctrl**> key and move the cursor over **Tutankhamun** in the **Navigation Bar**. The cursor changes to a pointing hand, indicating a **Link**.

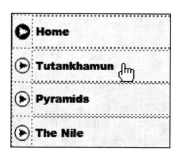

10.   Click to display page **2**. The **Navigation Bar** has been added to this page automatically. Drag it to the same position that it occupies on page **1**.

11.   Use the **Navigation Bar** to display page **3** then reposition the **Navigation Bar**. Repeat for page **4**.

12.   Use the **Navigation Bar** to display the **Home** page, page **1**.

13.   Save the **egypt** publication and leave it open.

# Exercise 41 - Web Hyperlinks

### Knowledge:

Regular users of the **Internet** will be familiar with hyperlinks - they allow a new page or location to be displayed, with a click of the mouse.

Hyperlinks can be used to navigate around a Web site, to other sites, to e-mail addresses or to other accessible files. Hyperlinks can be added manually to any text or object in a publication.

### Activity:

1.    On page **1** of the **egypt** publication, draw a text box (18cm wide by 1cm high) below the map.

2.    Enter the text **This site developed by Big Planet. You can send your comments here**. Apply **Best Fit**.

3.    Highlight the text **Big Planet** and select **Insert | Hyperlink**. Make sure **Existing File or Web Page** is selected on the left.

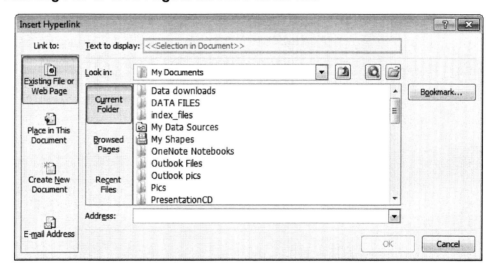

4.    Type **www.bigplanetsupport.co.uk** in the **Address** box.

5.    Click **OK**. Notice the selected text has changed colour, indicating that it is now a hyperlink.

6.    Highlight the text **here** and select **Insert | Hyperlink**.

7.    Select **E-mail Address** on the left. In the **E-mail address** box type **trainer@bigplanetsupport.co.uk**. Type **Egypt** in the **Subject** box. Click **OK**.

8.    Hyperlinks can be checked as before. Hold down the **<Ctrl>** key and move the cursor over the **Big Planet** text.

9.    Click to open the **Big Planet Support** web site in your browser application (if you have a currently active **Internet** connection).

10.   Close your browser application but leave the publication open for the next exercise.

# Exercise 42 - Animations

### Knowledge:

Moving images can be added to a web page to make it more dynamic and appealing to the viewer. *Publisher 2007* comes with a limited supply of "animated images", which are available from the clip art gallery. To access the full library of animated and clip art images an Internet connection is necessary. This allows *Office* applications to connect to *Microsoft Office Online* and download material from the web. Without an active Internet connection, it is unlikely that a suitable gallery of animated images will be available.

### Activity:

1. Display page **4** of the **egypt** publication and select **Insert | Picture | Clip Art**.

2. The Clip Art task pane is displayed. Search for **Egypt**, specifying that the search should be in **All collections** (select **Everywhere** from the drop down list if necessary).

3. Use the drop down list for **Results should be** and make sure the media file type of **Movies** is selected. Click **Go**.

4. A star symbol on a clip,  , indicates that it is animated. Click on the following clip, or an alternative animation if this clip is unavailable.

5. Enlarge the image to about **200px** wide and centre it below the heading text box.

| Note: | Make sure that no objects on the page overlap the animated image, or the clip may not be animated correctly. |
|---|---|

6. The animation will be demonstrated when the publication is previewed as a web page in a later exercise. Leave the publication open for the next exercise.

# Exercise 43 - Sounds

### Knowledge:

Any sound file can be added to a web page. The sound can either be looped continuously, or set to play for a specific number of times. Choose carefully when adding background sound, sometimes music on a web page can be irritating. You should also be aware of copyright issues when using sounds, especially music files which have been downloaded.

### Activity:

1.  Make sure page **1** of the **egypt** publication is selected.

2.  Locate the **Web Tools** toolbar and click **Background Sound**.

3.  In the **Web Page Options** dialog box, click the **Browse** button in the **Background sound** area.

4.  The **Background Sound** dialog box appears. By default the **Pub60COR** folder should be displayed, which is part of the **Clip Art** collection of images and sounds that are supplied with *Microsoft Office*. Select the **EAST_01** file and click **Open**.

> **Note:** *If you cannot access this folder, a copy of the **EAST_01** file has been included in the supplied data folder.*

5.  Select the **Loop forever** option so that the sound will play for as long as the site is open.

6.  Click **OK** to apply the sound.

> **Note:** *The sound will only play on the selected page of the website. The computer must have speakers or the music will not be audible.*

7.  The sounds will be demonstrated when the publication is previewed as a web page in the next exercise. Save the **egypt** publication and leave it open.

# Exercise 44 - Web Page Preview

### Knowledge:

A web publication can be viewed as it would be seen on the Internet whilst it is still a publisher file by using the **Web Page Preview** feature.

A web browser such as *Internet Explorer* must be installed on the computer before the **Web Page Preview** will work.

### Activity:

1.  Display page **1** of the **egypt** publication.

2.  Select **File | Web Page Preview** or click **Web Page Preview**, [icon], from the **Web Tools** toolbar.

3.  Your web browser application will start and will display the publication as it will appear on the Internet. Maximise the screen if necessary. If your computer has any sound capability, the attached sound file will start playing.

*This screenshot is taken using Internet Explorer 8*

4.  Scroll down the page to the text below the map. Click on **Big Planet** to open the site then click the **Back** button on your browser to return.

5.  Click the word **here** to open your e-mail application with a message ready to be completed. Close the e-mail application without saving anything.

6.  Scroll up and click the **Pyramids** link in the **Navigation Bar**. The **Pyramids** page is displayed.

7.  Click **The Nile** link to display that page. The animation will play once. To see it again, click the **Refresh** button in your browser.

8.  Click the **Home** link to return to the first page. Close your browser but leave the publication open.

# Exercise 45 - Save as Web Page

### Knowledge:

You have seen how web pages created and displayed in *Publisher* may be previewed in a web browser. To enable web pages to be opened directly in a web browser without requiring *Publisher* at all, the web publication may be saved as html documents using **File | Save As**.

### Activity:

1.  With the **egypt** publication open, select **File | Save As** to display the **Save As** dialog box.

2.  Enter **egyptweb** as the filename and select **Web Page, Filtered (*.htm;*.html)** as the file type to save.

3.  Ensure that the contents of the supplied data folder are displayed in the dialog box and click **Save**.

4.  Close *Publisher*.

5.  Use *Windows* to view the contents of the **Documents** library/folder and navigate to the supplied data folder. Amongst the other files will be a **egyptweb** folder and an **egyptweb** html file.

6.  Double click on the **egyptweb** html file (the folder contains all the components for the web site).

7.  The web site is displayed in your browser. *Publisher* is not active. Display each page using the **Navigation Bar** then close the browser and *Windows Explorer*.

# Exercise 46 - Web Site Template

### Knowledge:

Another option for producing a publication to be viewed in a web browser is to create a publication based on a **Web Site** template.

### Activity:

1.  Start *Publisher,* and select **Web Sites** from the **Getting Started** window

2.  Select the **Tabs** design and click **Create**. The **Easy Web Site Builder** dialog box is displayed.

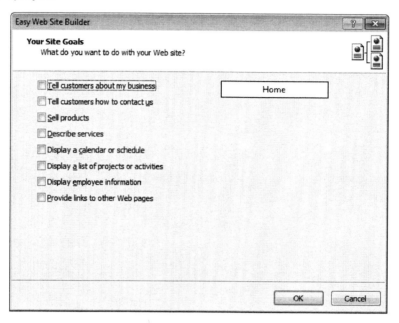

3.  Look at the options available then click the first two options to select them. This will add two extra pages to the publication. Click **OK**. A three page publication is built. The **Title Bar** indicates that it is a **Web Publication**. The content can now be changed to suit your own requirements.

> **Note:**   *Most objects can be manipulated in the same way as for **Print Publications**, although some formatting features may not be available.*

4.  Select **File | Web Page Preview**. After a short preparation process, your Internet Browser application will start and the publication will be displayed.

5.  Use the **Navigation** buttons on the left to move between the three pages, and use the scroll bars to move up and down each page.

6.  Close the browser by clicking the close button in the top right corner of the window, then close the publication <u>without</u> saving.

# Exercise 47 - Develop Your Skills

You will find a *Develop Your Skills* exercise at the end of each Skill Set. Work through it to ensure you've understood the previous exercises.

1.  Create a blank **Web Sites** publication, size. **Web 984 x 4608px**. Use **Tools | Options | General** and make sure the measurement units are set to **Pixels**.

2.  Set all **Margin Guides** for the page to **50px**.

3.  Draw a text box on the page, **250px** high and **500px** wide. Move it to the top right corner of the margins. Type **Bathroom Designs** in the text box, apply **Best Fit**, and change the font to **Verdana**, **Italic**.

4.  Format the text box to have a dark blue border and a pale blue fill.

5.  Display the **Clip Art** task pane and insert an animated image (Movie) using a search criteria of **bath**. Use an alternative animated image if necessary.

6.  Size the image to about **100px** square and move it to the lower right corner of the text box.

7.  Apply a background **Texture fill (Water droplets)** to the page.

8.  Draw a text box on the page below the first text box, **80px** high and the width of the margins. Fill it with pale green. Type **Home** in the text box, change the font to **36pt** and centre it.

9.  Insert a **Navigation Bar** using the **Dimension** style. Move it to the upper left of the page.

10. Add three more pages to the publication. Duplicate all objects from the current page and make sure hyperlinks for the new pages are automatically added to the navigation bars.

11. Change the **Home** text to **Designs**, **Prices** and **Order** on pages **2**, **3** and **4** respectively.

12. Change the display text on the navigation bar buttons to **Home**, **Designs**, **Prices** and **Order** .

13. Add a sound file to play forever when the web site is opened (**CARBN_01.MID** is suitable, or if none is available use the supplied file, **EAST_01.MID**).

14. Preview the publication in a browser and check that the navigation buttons function correctly then close the browser.

15. Save the publication as a **Filtered Web Page** with a name of **bathweb** and close it.

---

**Note:** *An example solution is shown in the **Answers** at the end of the guide.*

---

# Summary: Web Publications

In this Skill Set you have seen some of the principles of creating and formatting publications to be used as Web pages, including using web site templates.

You have seen how to use various components specifically designed for Web Publications such as Navigation bars, sounds and animations.

You have also learnt how to preview your Web publication and how to save it in the correct format.

Your OCR ITQ evidence must demonstrate your ability to:

- Select and use appropriate media for the publication

# Skill Set 8

# Design

By the end of this Skill Set you should be able to:

Recognise Practical Publication

Understand Publication Styles

Understand Publication Schemes

Understand Publication Layout

Use Preset Business Information

# Exercise 48 - Practical Publications

### Knowledge:

The techniques and features which have been described in previous skill sets, can all be combined in the creation of practical publications which may be used for a variety of purposes.

A good way to see this is to look at some publications which have been created from supplied *Publisher* templates.

### Activity:

1. Select **File | Open**. Locate the supplied data folder and open the **Sample2** publication. This publication was based on one of the **Brochure** templates.

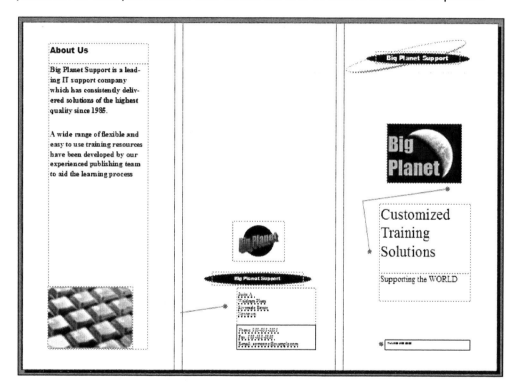

2. Look at the **Format Publication** task pane. The publication is based on a template using the **Arcs** design and is intended to be printed on **A4** paper in **Landscape** orientation.

3. This is a two page publication. Click on the icon for page **2**. The second page is displayed.

> **Note:** The two pages of the publication are meant to be printed on either side of a single sheet of paper, which can then be folded vertically into a six part brochure.

4. Move the cursor over both pages of the publication. Many of the objects and features described in the guide can be found here.

# Exercise 48 - Continued

5. See if you can find examples of:

   Text Boxes

   Pictures

   Tables

   Ovals

   AutoShapes

   Lines

   Text Wrapping

   Object 'Stacking'

   Grouping

6. Open the **Sample3** publication.

---

**Note:** *The shuttle animation is included courtesy of NASA.*

---

7. Look at the **Title Bar**. It shows the text **Web Publication**. This publication has been created using a **Web Site** template, designed to be shown as a series of web pages.

8. Look at the **Web Site Options** panel on the left. As the publication is meant to be viewed on a scrollable web browser display rather than in print, the page size is long and narrow and is shown in **pixels** (**px**), the units of screen display size.

9. Move the cursor over different objects on the first page. The usual objects such as **Text Box**, **Picture** and **Shape** can be found, along with some new ones such as the **Navigation Bar** with its hyperlinks (on the left). These were added automatically as part of the template.

10. To see how the publication will appear as a web page, display the **File** menu and select **Web Page Preview**. After a short preparation process, your Internet Browser application will start and the publication will be displayed.

11. As the publication is designed to be viewed as a web page, it can include multimedia components. Notice that one of the pictures on the first page is an animation. If your computer can play sounds, you will hear that a short sound clip has been attached to the publication.

12. Check the navigation button operation the close the browser.

13. Open the **Sample1** publication. This was created using one of the **Business Card** templates.

14. Leave all publications open.

# Exercise 49 - Design Styles

### Knowledge:

The three sample publications seen in previous exercises have all had a consistent appearance, even though their function has been quite different. For many organisations, a consistent appearance to all documents and visual displays is a requirement as it can create an integrated, professional image. Many organisations will therefore impose a 'house style' to be used for all output that they produce. In large organisations, different imposed styles may be defined for individual products or brands to help create a 'brand identity'.

The definition of a house style will vary from organisation to organisation, but will normally include some or all of the following:

| | |
|---|---|
| **Font Schemes** | Fonts can be very powerful in setting a consistent image and some large companies will even create their own unique fonts. Most house styles will specify the fonts to be used. |
| **Colour Schemes** | Similarly, the consistent use of colour can help to define a strong identity. Font colour is particularly important. |
| **Pictures** | Although different pictures will be required in different publications, the use of some standard images (logos for example) and individual graphic designs (shapes) can help create a consistent style. |
| **Layout** | Again the overall layout of individual publications will need to vary but some rules can be specified, such as the alignment of text, and the positioning of titles, pictures and white space. |

Other guidelines may exist locally to specify what content should or should not be included. These may be based on cultural or ethnic considerations.

### Activity:

1. The publications **Sample1**, **Sample2** and **Sample3** have a consistent appearance even though they are different types of publications. Display the **Sample1** publication. It is a **Business Card** type of publication.

2. Click **Business Card Options** in the **Format Publication** task pane if it is not already displayed. The publication is based on a template which uses the **Arcs** design. All three sample publications are based on this design.

3. Click **Color Schemes** in the **Format Publication** task pane. The selected color scheme is **Rain Forest**. All publications use the same color scheme.

4. Click **Font Schemes** in the **Format Publication** task pane. All publications use the same **Business Card Template** font scheme.

5. Look at the **Big Planet** logo. All three publications use this image.

6. Leave all publications open.

# Exercise 50 - Colour Schemes

### Knowledge:

Colours can make a big difference to the appearance of publications even though the content and layout stays the same. All colours on a page can be changed manually, but using one of the supplied colour schemes should guarantee that all the colours used will be a pleasing combination.

### Activity:

1. Display the **Sample2** publication.

**Note:** *Sample2 should be on the list of **Recent Publications**, displayed on the right of the **Getting Started** screen. Click on it here to open it.*

2. Click **Color Schemes** in the **Task Pane**, 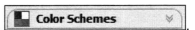.

3. Note that the currently selected scheme is **Rain Forest**. This is the same scheme used in **Sample1** and **Sample3**, which helps to give them all a consistent appearance

4. Scroll up the list and select **Cherry**.

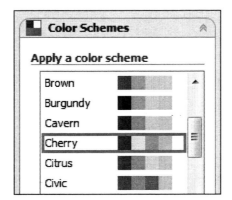

5. The colour of the main text and of all graphics (shapes, lines and borders) in this publication is changed, resulting in a completely different look to the pages.

6. Try selecting different color schemes to see the effect.

7. Finally select the **Flow** scheme.

8. Leave all publications open.

# Exercise 51 - Font Schemes

### Knowledge:

Fonts can be a distinctive feature of publications and a consistent use of fonts can help to provide a recognisable style. They can make a big difference to the appearance of publications even though the content and layout stays the same.

### Activity:

1.  In the **Sample2** publication, click **Font Schemes** in the **Task Pane**.

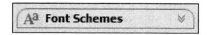

2.  Scroll down and select the **Binary** theme which uses the **Verdana** font for titles and headings and the **Georgia** font for other text. All fonts in this publication are changed.

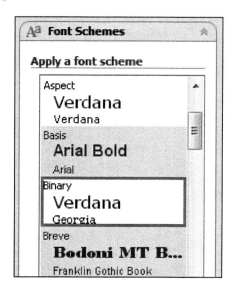

3.  Click in the word **Customized** in the right panel of the page. The font information on the **Formatting** toolbar shows that this is **Verdana**.

4.  Click in a text paragraph in the left panel of the page. The font information on the **Formatting** toolbar shows that this is **Georgia**.

5.  Close all publications <u>without</u> saving.

# Exercise 52 - Layout

### Knowledge:

The design of individual page layouts can make a big difference to the effectiveness of a publication. Decisions must also be made as to exactly what information needs to appear. Consider the purpose of the publication and ensure that all of the necessary information required to meet that purpose is included.

The actual positioning, sizing, proportion and formatting of objects will be covered in a later exercise, but the effects will be demonstrated here. Creating an effective design for a publication, taking into account all the points mentioned here, can be a specialist skill and many companies and individuals are available to provide such expertise at a cost. For the amateur, it may be as well to base publications on one of the many pre-designed templates which are available in *Publisher*.

### Activity:

1. Open the **Day1** publication. This is simple, single page **Quick Publication** type of publication based on the **Arcs** design template. Note the design is quite sparse with lots of space on the page with no content. This is known as **white space** and can make a page more striking, particularly if the publication is meant to be eye-catching.

2. Open the **Day2** publication. This is the same publication with the objects moved and resized and some extra detail added to fill the page. This is basically the same content but with quite a different look. Which type of design best fits your requirements may be influenced by company guidelines or personal choice, or by the intended audience.

*Day1*

*Day2*

# Exercise 52 - Continued

3.     Close both publications.

4.     Suppose you need to create a company newsletter. From the **Getting Started** screen, click **Newsletters**, either on the main screen or on the left panel.

5.     There is a range of different template designs which can be used as the basis for your publication. Select the first one, **Arrows**, and click the **Create** button.

6.     The publication template is displayed, ready for you to add your own content. The design shows some subtle graphics, text displayed in columns and plenty of white space to balance the page layout.

> **Note:**   *Do not ignore white space in the design of pages – it can be a useful component of a good design.*

7.     Open the publication **News2**. This is basically the same publication design but with more information squeezed onto the page. It could be argued that this leads to a less attractive publication.

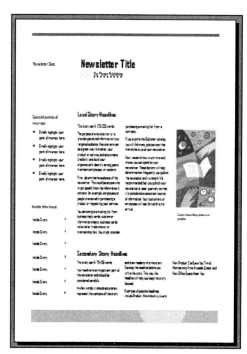 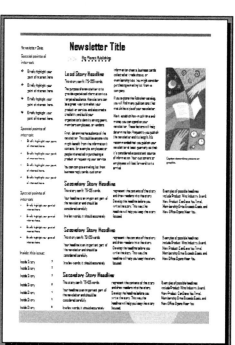

*Original Template*                  *News2*

> **Note:**   *When designing a new publication, spend some time considering the layout of the page – images and text need to be positioned to achieve a suitable balanced design that is appealing to your intended audience.*

8.     Close both publications.

# Exercise 53 - Business Information

### Knowledge:

*Publisher 2007* has a feature which allows certain personal information to be defined, which is then included in any publication created from a template. This is called **Business Information** and it can be edited to suit your own needs.

### Activity:

1.    Open the **Sample1** publication. This business card was created from a template and all the text and the company logos were automatically added from **Business Information**.

2.    Select **Edit | Business Information**. If no **Business Information** has been entered yet, the following dialog box will be displayed.

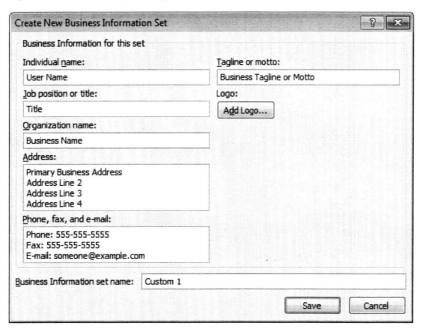

| Note: | *If a set of information has already been entered, the **Business Information** dialog box will be displayed and you will have to click **Edit** to change it, or **New** to add a new set of information.* |
|---|---|

3.    Enter your own personal or company details. If a logo is currently displayed, click the **Remove** button and then click **Yes**.

4.    Click **Add Logo** to display the **Insert Picture** dialog box. Select the supplied **Logo1** file and click **Insert**.

5.    Click **Save**.

6.    In the **Business Information** dialog box, click **Update Publication**. The publication now shows the amended information, and the next time a *Publisher* template is opened, the new information will be used.

7.    Close the publication without saving.

# Exercise 54 - Develop Your Skills

You will find a *Develop Your Skills* exercise at the end of each Skill Set. Work through it to ensure you've understood the previous exercises.

1.　Open the **Tournament** publication.

2.　Can you find examples of text boxes, pictures and drawn shapes (**AutoShapes**) on the page? Move the cursor over the page and check the tooltips for confirmation.

3.　What other type of object can be found on the page?

4.　What is white space and why can it be important?

5.　What type of publication is this?

6.　Which design template is the publication based on?

7.　What page orientation is applied?

8.　Click in the main title. Which font is used?

9.　Click in the table. Which font is used here?

10.　Which **Color Scheme** is used?

11.　Change it to **Citrus**.

12.　Close the publication <u>without</u> saving.

13.　**Exit** *Publisher*.

| Note: | The answers are listed in the **Answers** section at the end of the guide. |
|---|---|

# Summary: Design

In this Skill Set you have seen some of the different types of publication available and some of the objects that can be added to the pages.

You have also seen some of the features such as font and colour that affect design and page layout of publications and learned why set design schemes (house styles) may be imposed by organisations on all of their publications

<u>Your OCR ITQ evidence must demonstrate your ability to:</u>

- Describe what types of information are needed, including:
  - Text
  - Images
  - Graphics
  - Video
  - Sound

- Select, change and use page design and layout in line with any local guidelines, including the use of:
  - Data organisation
  - Styles
  - Colours
  - Font schemes
  - White space
  - Consistency
  - Orientation
  - House styles and guidelines

- Select and use appropriate media for the presentation, including:
  - Printed document
  - Web page
  - Multimedia

# Skill Set 9

# Finishing

By the end of this Skill Set you should be able to:

Create Templates

Use Print Setup

Print and Print Preview

Check Publications

Save Publications

Save Images

Recognise File Types

# Exercise 55 - Creating Templates

### Knowledge:

Having created a satisfactory page layout, you may wish to be able to use this again to create other publications. The best way to do this is to create a template.

### Activity:

1. Create a blank **A4 (Portrait)** publication.

2. Select **Arrange | Layout** guides and set the **Grid Guides** to **2** columns and **3** rows with the default spacing.

3. Select **Insert | Picture** and insert the file **Logo1** from the supplied data. Move the picture to the top right corner of the margin guides.

4. Draw a text box filling the middle left cell of the layout guides (use inner lines).

5. Insert the file **Orchids** from the supplied data. Move the picture to the lower right corner of the margin guides.

6. The picture should overlap the text box. Select **Arrange | Order | Send to Back** to make sure any text in the text box will be seen on top of the picture.

7. Select **File | Save As** to display the **Save As** dialog box.

8. Change the **File name** to **Notes**, then click the drop down arrow on the **Save as type** box and select **Publisher Template**.

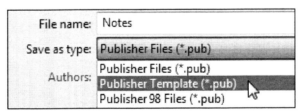

9. When **Publisher Template** is selected, the location for the saved file automatically changes to the **Templates** folder.

10. Click **Save**, then close the publication.

11. In the *Publisher* **Getting Started** window, click **My Templates** on the left. All your saved templates will be shown here.

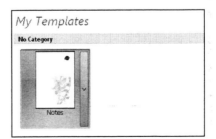

12. Use the **Back** button to return to the **Getting Started** window.

# Exercise 56 - Print Setup

### Knowledge:

A finished publication may need printing. Before printing however, it is possible to define some settings which will control how the print is produced.

### Activity:

1.  Open the **MyCard** publication and select **File | Print Setup**. As the business card layout is small, the default is to produce many copies on one **A4** sheet.

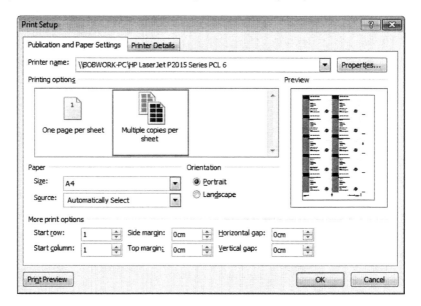

2.  Make sure the correct printer is selected in **Printer name**. Different printers will allow different effects, e.g. some printers will not show a colour preview.

3.  Set the **Orientation** to **Landscape** (this is the paper orientation only).

4.  Click the **Print Preview** button to see how final print will look. Notice there may be some extra information printed, such as short horizontal and vertical lines which tell the user where to cut the sheet to create the right size items.

5.  Click **Close** to return to the **Print Setup** dialog box.

6.  Click **One page per sheet**. Larger pages will only have this option.

7.  Click **OK** then close the publication without saving.

# Exercise 57 - Printing

### *Knowledge:*

A print out from a publication can take many forms. However, you will only need to print out a "composite proof". This means that all items, in all colours that appear on the page, will appear on a single print.

It is important to be aware of the difference between publication pages and printed pages. As seen in the previous exercise, more than one publication can be printed on a single sheet of A4 paper.

If the **Print** button, 🖨, is used, a single copy of the entire publication is printed.

### *Activity:*

1. Open the publication **Getwell**. Notice the publication page size (as shown in the task pane) is **10.5 x 14.85cm**.

2. Select **File | Print** to display the **Print** dialog box.

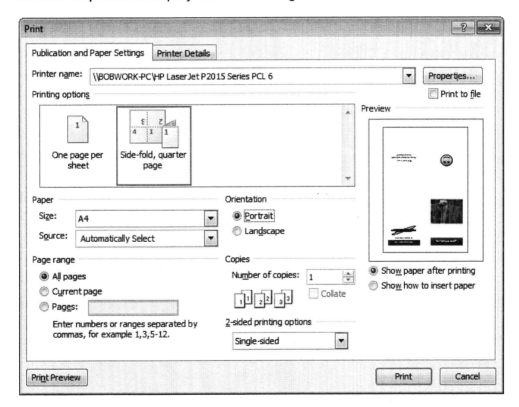

3. The top part of this dialog box is the **Print Setup** information, and the lower part has settings such as **Number of copies** and which **Range** of pages to print. Make sure the **Paper Size** is **A4** (21 x 29.7cm).

4. As all four publisher pages will fit on one **A4** sheet (in **Portrait** orientation), and because publisher knows that this is a greeting card design, a special printing option is shown as the default. Click **Print Preview** to see it more clearly.

# Exercise 57 - Continued

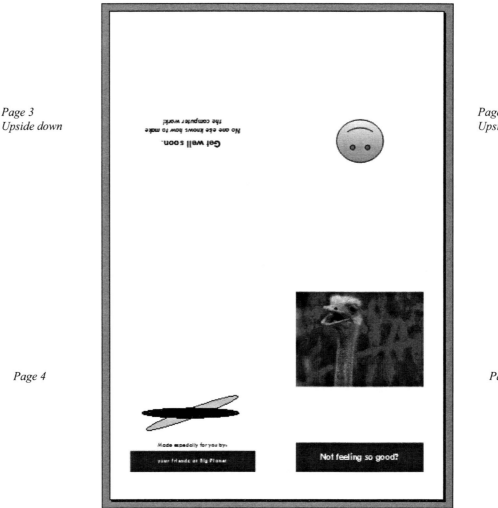

*Page 3*
*Upside down*

*Page 2*
*Upside down*

*Page 4*

*Page 1*

5.     Click **Close** to close **Preview** and return to the **Print** dialog box. Click **Print** to print a copy of the publication as shown in the preview.

6.     Take the printed sheet and fold it in half horizontally, then fold the result in half vertically (with the ostrich on the outside). You will have your very own greeting card.

7.     Select **File | Print** again and select **One page per sheet**. With the **Page range** set to **All pages**, click **Print**. Four sheets will be printed with a page on each.

8.     Click the **Print** button, ⎙, on the **Standard** toolbar. This will also print one copy of the publication in the default mode with no further prompting.

9.     Close the publication <u>without</u> saving.

# Exercise 58 - Publication Checking

### Knowledge:

Once a publication has been completed, it should be checked. Aspects such as accuracy of information and completeness are important and must be checked manually, possibly with the help of people not connected with its creation.

Appearance is also very important and should be checked to make sure it is suitable for its intended purpose. Areas to check could include:

- Orientation of pages and objects

- Formatting and alignment of text

- Quality of images

- Layout of objects on the page

- Use of colour

*Publisher* does, however, have features which help the checking process in certain areas.

### Activity:

1.  Open the publication **Sample2**. In a practical situation the publication would be checked manually to ensure that it met any house style rules, contained accurate information, and met the purpose for which it was designed.

2.  Although there is a spell checking option in *Publisher*, it is more appropriate to use the more comprehensive features of *Word*. Switch to page **2** of the publication and click in the text box on the centre panel.

3.  Select **Edit | Edit Story in Microsoft Word**. Your copy of *Word* will be started and the text from the text box will be displayed as a document. Notice that the **Task Bar** contains the word count for this text.

4.  Select the **Review** tab on the **Ribbon** at the top of the *Word* window, then select **Spelling & Grammar**.

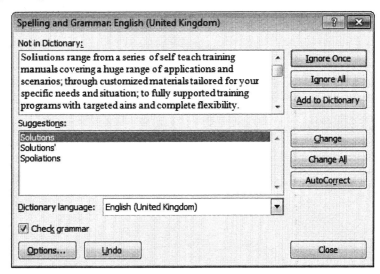

# Exercise 58 - Continued

5.   The first **Suggestions** option is correct (**Solutions**). Click **Change**.

6.   At the next spelling check (**ains**) click **Change** again.

7.   The next issue is a grammar check. Again accept the suggested option by clicking **Change**.

8.   Click **OK** at the check complete message.

> **Note:**   *Spell checkers only identify words they don't recognise, not words that are misused. Always proof read your text manually.*

9.   Click the **Office Button** in the top left of the *Word* window and select **Close & Return to Sample2** to return to *Publisher* with the text corrected. Remember to change the zoom setting if necessary to refresh the view.

10.  For more help with checking, select **Tools | Design Checker** to display the **Design Checker** task pane.

> **Note:**   *Only general design checks are run by default.*

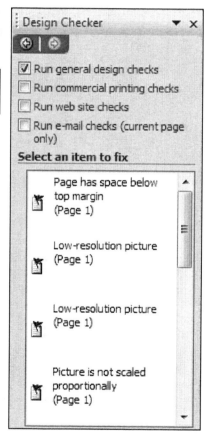

11.  Click each item identified in the **Design Checker** task pane. The offending item in the publication is selected automatically.

12.  To find out more about a particular error type, and learn ways to fix the problem, click the drop-down arrow to the right of an item and select **Explain**.

13.  *Publisher's* **Help** window will open. Once you have read about the issue, close the **Help** window to return to the publication.

14.  Select **Tools | Graphics Manager** to display the **Graphics Manager** task pane. This gives details of all graphic files that have been inserted. Notice that the pictures come from different file types such as **.gif**, **.png** and **.bmp**.

15.  Finally, manually check the whole document by reading all of the text carefully. For your own publications you will need to check if the text is accurate and complete. Are there any ways that formatting or layout could be improved? Is all content clear, with nothing indistinct or hidden? Are there any colour combinations which could be difficult to resolve?

16.  Save the publication as **sample2 fixed** and close it.

# Exercise 59 - File Types

### Knowledge:

Any publication must be saved if it is to be used again. In previous exercises, files have been saved to the supplied data folder as normal *Publisher* files and as *Publisher* templates. It is possible to save publications as other file types and to specific locations.

### Activity:

1.  Open the **Getwell** publication, select the **File** menu and choose the **Save As** command. The **Save As** dialog box will then appear.

2.  The dialog box should display the contents of the supplied data folder (if not, locate it now). Enter **test** in the **File name** box.

3.  Click the drop down arrow to the right of the **Save as type** box. A list of all available file types is displayed.

| Publisher Files (*.pub) |
|---|
| Publisher Template (*.pub) |
| Publisher 98 Files (*.pub) |
| Publisher 2000 Files (*.pub) |
| Unicode Text Files (*.txt) |
| PostScript (*.ps) |
| PDF (*.pdf) |
| XPS Document (*.xps) |
| Plain Text (*.txt) |
| Single File Web Page (*.mht;*.mhtml) |
| Web Page, Filtered (*.htm;*.html) |
| Rich Text Format (*.rtf) |
| Works 6.0 - 9.0 (*.wps) |
| Word 2007 Macro-enabled Document |
| Works 6 - 9 Document (*.wps) |
| Word 2007 Document (*.docx) |
| Word 97-2003 Document (*.doc) |
| GIF Graphics Interchange Format (*.gif) |
| JPEG File Interchange Format (*.jpg) |
| Tag Image File Format (*.tif) |
| PNG Portable Network Graphics Format |
| Device Independent Bitmap (*.bmp) |
| Windows Metafile (*.wmf) |
| Enhanced Metafile (*.emf) |

**Note:** *Many of the file types available are meant to be used in different applications and cannot themselves be opened by Publisher.*

4.  Select **PDF** from the list.

5.  It is possible here to create a new folder to contain your file – the **Save As** dialog box has a **New folder** button. Click this to create a folder with a highlighted name of **New folder**.

6.  Type **Extra** and press **<Enter>**.

7.  Click **Open**, to open the new folder and then **Save**, to save the file. A file called **test.pdf** will be saved in the **Extra** folder (it may automatically open).

8.  Use *Windows Explorer* to view the supplied data folder. The folder will now contain a subfolder called **Extra**.

| Name | Date modified | Type | Size |
|---|---|---|---|
| extra | 20/11/2010 11:50 | File folder | |
| Business1.pub | 12/11/2010 08:52 | Microsoft Office Publisher ... | 97 KB |
| Canyon.docx | 12/11/2010 14:42 | Microsoft Office Word Do... | 16 KB |

**Note:** *You can switch to **Details** view to see the size of all files. If publishing to the Internet, it is advisable to keep file sizes as low as possible.*

9.  Close the *Windows Explorer* window and return to *Publisher*.

10.  Close the publication (and the PDF document, if applicable) <u>without</u> saving.

# Exercise 60 - Save as Picture

### Knowledge:

There are many different file types available for image files, with each one having specific features depending on how the image is to be used.

Individual objects in a publication can be saved as images, and complete publication pages, however complex, can be saved as a single picture. This picture could then be used anywhere a picture can be used, for example as an Internet display. The best choice of file type will be determined by the intended use for the picture.

### Activity:

1.      Open the **Day2** publication.

2.      The whole page is to be saved as an image. Select **File | Save As**.

3.      In the **Save As** dialog box change the **File name** to **page**.

4.      Click the drop down on the **Save as type** box to see the available formats. The last seven options are image file types.

> GIF Graphics Interchange Format (*.gif)
> JPEG File Interchange Format (*.jpg)
> Tag Image File Format (*.tif)
> PNG Portable Network Graphics Format (*.png)
> Device Independent Bitmap (*.bmp)
> Windows Metafile (*.wmf)
> Enhanced Metafile (*.emf)

5.      Select the **JPEG** type.

| Note: | The JPEG file format is ideal for storing pictures. As it is compressed, it is quick to download via the Internet and can be viewed in all web browsers. |
|---|---|

6.      As the file type is an image file, a **Change** option is shown in the dialog box (which lets you change the **resolution** of the image).

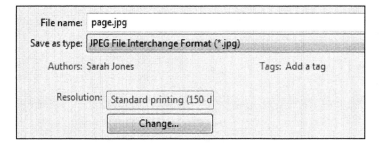

7.      Click **Change**. The **Change Resolution** dialog box is displayed.

| Note: | An image's resolution in this case refers to its print size and not how it appears on a computer screen. In very simple terms, the higher the resolution, the bigger and more detailed the image will appear when printed. |
|---|---|

# Exercise 60 - Continued

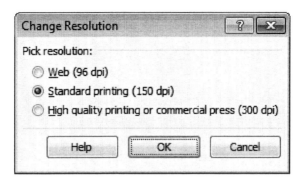

8.  It is possible to change the resolution of the image (and hence the file size) from here. Select **Web (96 dpi)** and click **OK**. Click **Save**.

9.  Any individual object on the page, such as text box, picture or shape, can be saved as an image file.

10. Right click in the main title text, **Open Day**, and select **Save as Picture**.

11. The **Save As** dialog box is displayed. If necessary, navigate to the supplied data folder.

12. The default **File name** will be **Picture1**. Change it to **page title**.

13. Click the drop down on the **Save as type** box. Only image file types are shown. Select **PNG** type and click **Save**.

> **Note:** *The PNG file format – as with the GIF and TIF formats – are ideal for storing small, simple graphic files. They do not lose quality as much as a JPEG, but this results in much larger file sizes. They are also common web formats that can be viewed in most web browsers.*

14. Use *Windows Explorer* to view the supplied data folder. Both images will be listed. The view below is **Large Icons** in *Windows 7*.

> **Note:** *BMP files are typically used to store "raw" images (without compression). However, their large file size make them unsuitable for use on the Internet. Other file formats are also available to save in, but these are outside the scope of this guide.*

15. Close the *Windows Explorer* window and return to *Publisher.* Close the **Day2** publication <u>without</u> saving.

# Exercise 61 - File Type Considerations

### Knowledge:

As you learned in the previous exercise, when saving a publication, different file types should be used for different purposes. The **format** you choose will directly affect how easy the final publication can be used: how good it will look when viewed or printed; how much disk space it will take up; how quickly it can be transmitted by e-mail; and how fast can it be download from a website.

Some file types will **compress** the contents of your publication. These files are usually easier to share with others, but there is always a trade-off between image quality and file size. Generally speaking, the higher the quality, the larger the size of the file and the longer it will take to transmit electronically (and vice versa). You will need to find a balance that most suits your publication's final purpose.

Some of the main file formats *Publisher* can save publications in are listed below:

- **BMP**　　**Bitmap**. Files of this type contain raw, uncompressed image data. They represent the maximum image quality, but also the largest file size.

- **JPG**　　Pronounced **J-PEG**, this is a file format most commonly used to store digital photographs. Images are compressed, but the degree of compression can be adjusted when you save the file – the higher the compression, the smaller the file size and the lower the image quality.

- **PNG**　　**Portable Network Graphic**. Pronounced **PING**, these are files that are compressed automatically, but without loss of quality. They are useful for simple graphics distributed via the web. The compression used is very limited however, and so large PNG files will have large file sizes.

- **GIF**　　**Graphics Interchange Format**. Similar to PNG, this is an older file format used for simple web graphics. However, images are limited to a small set of colours (which will often the affect the look of the image).

- **TIF**　　**Tagged Image File Format**. This type of file is popular with professional desktop publishers and graphic artists. It is very similar to PNG, but uses better compression.

- **WMF**　　**Windows Meta File**. This file format is useful for saving images in a form ready to be used in other *Microsoft Office* products. Clip Art files are often distributed in WMF format.

- **PDF**　　**Portable Document Format**. This file type is very useful for creating a print-ready document to send to others. Once in this format, images can't easily be changed or edited.

Other types of file format you may encounter <u>outside</u> of *Publisher* are those produced by **vector** image programs. Unlike the above **raster** file types (in which pictures are composed of many coloured **pixels**), vector images are created using simple shapes, lines and fills, and can therefore produce very small file sizes.

# Exercise 62 - Develop Your Skills

You will find a *Develop Your Skills* exercise at the end of each Skill Set. Work through it to ensure you've understood the previous exercises.

1.   Open the publication **Sample2**.

2.   Select **File | Print**. The page fills one **A4** sheet in **Landscape** orientation.

3.   Select a **Paper Orientation** of **Portrait**. Why is this not a good idea? Select **Print Preview** to demonstrate.

4.   Close **Print Preview** and switch back to **Landscape** orientation.

5.   Print 1 copy of all pages.

6.   Close the publication without saving

7.   Open the publication **Check** and run the **Design Checker** tool. How many items are reported?

8.   Fix the text overflow item by enlarging the text box. Make sure the item disappears from the list.

9.   Edit the text in the text box in *Microsoft Word*.

10.  How many words are in the text?

11.  Run a spelling and grammar check. Locate and correct the two genuine spelling mistakes and one grammatical error. Ignore any names which are highlighted.

12.  Close *Microsoft Word*.

13.  List three more possible failings of the page.

14.  Select all of the text apart from the heading and justify it.

15.  Save the page as a single image named **skills9** suitable for displaying on the web.

16.  Use *Windows Explorer* to find the size of the saved file.

17.  Close the publication <u>without</u> saving.

| | |
|---|---|
| **Note:** | *Answers are shown in the **Answers** section at the end of the guide.* |

# Summary: Finishing

In this Skill Set you have seen how to use some of the tools available to preview and print simple publications. You have learned how to perform some checking techniques, including spelling and grammar checkers, and to recognise the importance of fully checking all completed publications.

You have also seen how to save objects or publications in a range of formats suitable for display in a variety of situations.

<u>Your OCR ITQ evidence must demonstrate your ability to:</u>

- Check publications meet needs, using IT tools and making corrections as necessary, including,
    - Spell check
    - Grammar check
    - Word count
    - Completeness
    - Accuracy
    - Formatting

- Identify and respond to quality problems:
    - Text clarity
    - Image clarity and content

# ITQ Assessment Criteria

| **C1** | **Select and use appropriate designs and page layouts for publications** | |
|---|---|---|
| 1.1 | Explain what types of information are needed | ☐ |
| 1.2 | Explain when and how to change page design and layout to increase the effectiveness of a publication | ☐ |
| 1.3 | Select, change, define, create and use an appropriate page design and layout for publications in line with local guidelines where relevant. | ☐ |
| 1.4 | Select and use appropriate media for the presentation. | ☐ |
| **C2** | **Input and combine text and other information within publications** | |
| 2.1 | Find and input information into publications so that it is ready for editing and formatting | ☐ |
| 2.2 | Organise and combine information for publications in line with copyright constraints, including importing information produced using other software | ☐ |
| 2.3 | Provide guidance on how copyright constraints affect use of own and others' information | ☐ |
| 2.4 | Explain which file format to use for saving designs and images | ☐ |
| 2.5 | Store and retrieve publication files effectively, in line with local guidelines and conventions where available | ☐ |
| **C3** | **Use desktop publishing software techniques to edit and format publications** | |
| 3.1 | Determine and discuss the styles colours, font schemes, editing and formatting to use for the publication | ☐ |
| 3.2 | Create styles, colours and font schemes to meet needs | ☐ |
| 3.4 | Manipulate images and graphic elements accurately | ☐ |
| 3.5 | Control text flow within single and multiple columns and pages | ☐ |
| 3.6 | Check publications meet needs, using IT tools, making corrections as necessary | ☐ |
| 3.6 | Identify and respond to quality problems with publications to make sure they are fit for purpose and meet needs | ☐ |

# Evidence Requirements

OCR has defined **Evidence Requirements** to meet the ITQ assessment criteria. A complete evidence checklist must be submitted with every unit to ensure all evidence required for the assessment and achievement of this unit has been produced.

> **Note:** *This unit can be achieved through one or more tasks.*

### C1   Select and use appropriate designs and page layouts for publications

At least four different types of information should be described.

The explanation should relate to three different publications.

There should be evidence (of using designs and layouts) from three different publications.

### C2   Input and combine text and other information within publications

There should be at least nine different examples of inputting, organising and combining information.

The candidate should store and retrieve at least six different file formats.

### C3   Use desktop publishing software techniques to edit and format publications

The candidate should justify their decisions (on styles, colours, fonts, editing and formatting). This can be supported by annotated sketches and/or screen images.

There should be nine different examples of editing, and three different examples of formatting.

There should be at least three different examples of checking publications. Examples of before and after amendments should be included

# Sample Scenarios

These suggested tasks are to help you develop your own ideas, which should be relevant to your own workplace (or workplace simulation). You could produce something similar to the suggestions below. *Please note that each task may not cover all evidence required for the unit in its own right.* Make sure that you obtain printouts and screen shots as you are creating your own publications, so that they can be used as ITQ evidence.

The various publications used in the course of this guide could all be adapted to be suitable types of task for this unit. Examine them to see if you could use the ideas within them to create your own solutions. It is essential that these examples are only used to show the sort of tasks that could be used. They must not be submitted in their own right.

## News Sheet

Create a news sheet about your organisation or club, or just about a topic that interests you. Include relevant articles and pictures of relevant objects, places or people.

## Poster

Create a poster to advertise a coming event such as a birthday party, football match or sponsored run. Include all relevant information such as times, dates, location. Use designs and colour to make the poster as eye-catching as possible.

## Web Page

Create a single web page to introduce a favourite holiday location. Use lots of relevant images and lots of references to places such as other web sites where more information can be viewed.

# Answers

Samples are displayed to demonstrate the publication layouts only.

## Exercise 7

3      **4** pages.

4      **Title Bar**, **Menu Bar**, several **Toolbars**.

5      **Task Pane**, **Objects Toolbar**.

8      **3** pages

12     **View | Task Pane**

13     **10 x 10.844cm**

15     **No**. The text 'wraps around' the picture

## Exercise 15

16     A new publication is started to contain the **Holiday** text.

## Exercise 20

12

**Exercise 29**

7

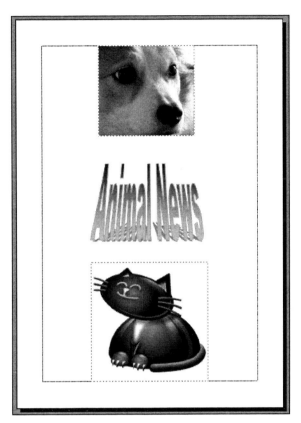

19　Some text is hidden behind the picture.

20　The text is now seen on top of the picture.

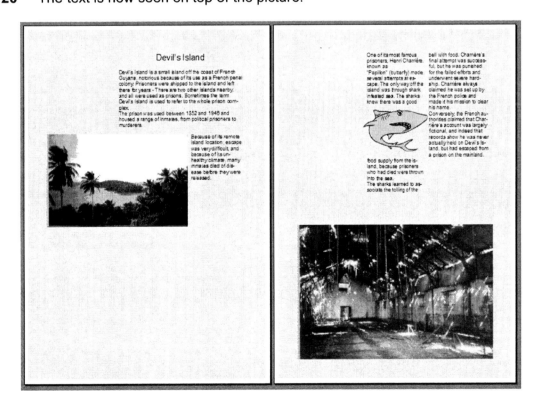

**Exercise 34**

5

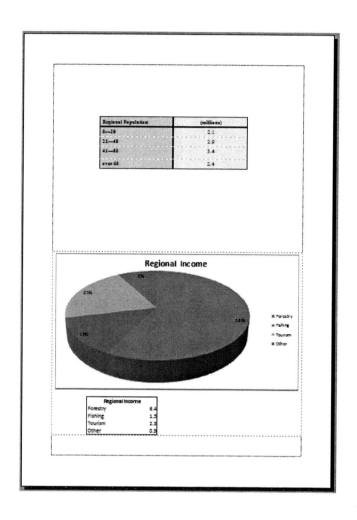

11    52%.

12    58%

**Exercise 38**

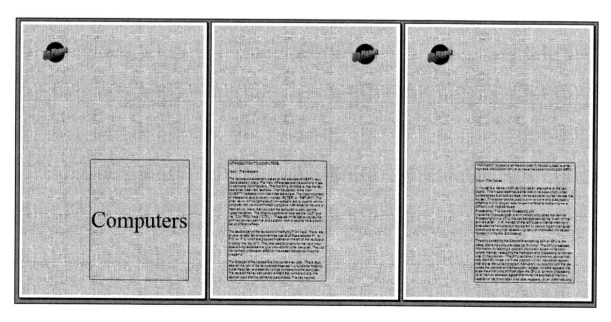

**Exercise 47**

**Exercise 54**

2      All 3 object types can be found.

3      **Table**

4      **White space** is space on the page that has no visible content.

         It can add to the balance and composition of the page layout.

5      **Flyer**

6      **Tilt**

7      **Portrait**

8      **Franklin Gothic Heavy**

9      **Gill Sans MT**

10     **Berry**

**Exercise 62**

3      It splits the document down the centre over two pages.

7      Maximum of 4 (some checks may not be activated on your system).

10     **238** words.

11     **peral**, **murdrers**, **was thrown**.

13     Page is generally dull

         Text untidy

         Heading not prominent

         Empty space at top looks unbalanced

         No use of colour

         Picture not relevant

16     51Kb

# Glossary

| | |
|---|---|
| **Best Fit** | A setting that will adjust the font size within a text frame so that all the text fits exactly into the available area. |
| **Clip Art** | A feature that gives access to the collection of images available within *Office*. |
| **Colour Scheme** | A predefined set of coordinated colours which can be used within a publication. |
| **Colour Separation Proof** | A printout where each colour used is printed on a separate page. |
| **Drag and Drop** | Moving an object by clicking on it and dragging to a new position. |
| **Fill Effects** | Effects that can be applied to any closed shape, such as a drawn circle or a text box. Effects include colour gradients, textures, patterns, pictures and tints. |
| **Font** | A type or style of print. |
| **Handles** | White circles that are displayed at the corners and at the centre of the sides of an object when it is selected. They can be used to resize the object. |
| **Import** | To insert text or pictures, which already exist in another location, into a publication. |
| **Indent** | An amount by which text is moved towards the vertical centre line of a page, away from a margin. |
| **Justified** | An alignment setting which straightens both the left and right margins of the text. |
| **Layout** | The arrangement of a publication to suit various purposes; **Special Fold** card, **Label**, **Envelope**, etc. |
| **Layout Guides** | Blue dotted lines around the page, which can help to line up objects on the page. |
| **Margin Guides** | Indicate the boundaries of the printed page. |
| **Object** | An item within a publication such as a picture or a text box. |
| **Objects Toolbar** | An extra toolbar, that by default is positioned down the left side of the screen, enabling the creation of various objects on the page. |

| | |
|---|---|
| **Orientation** | Whether the page is arranged horizontally or upright. |
| **Page Setup** | A facility that allows the layout and orientation of a publication to be specified. |
| **Picture Frame** | A frame that restricts the area in which a graphic image can be positioned and/or viewed. |
| **Point** | A unit of measurement of font size. 1 point equals 1/72 inch. |
| **Publication** | The universal name for a finished file created within *Publisher*. |
| **Sans Serif** | A style of font that does not have any decorative lines or curls on the "stalks" of letters. |
| **Select** | To highlight a section of text or click on an object to identify it for editing or formatting. |
| **Serif** | A style of font that has decorative lines or curls on the "stalks" of letters. |
| **Taskbar** | By default, a grey band across the bottom of the **Desktop**, which displays a button for each program that is currently running. |
| **Template** | A ready-made publication that requires only the text to be edited or a picture to be changed. |
| **Text Box** | A frame that restricts the area in which text can be typed and/or viewed. |
| **Text Flow** | Or **text wrap**: how text wraps around graphics. |
| **Text Wrapping** | The way text "flows" around a picture or other object positioned inside a text frame. |
| **Zoom** | A function that allows the degree of magnification of a page to be adjusted to suit the user. |

# Index

# Other Products from CiA Training

CiA Training is a leading publishing company which has consistently delivered the highest quality products since 1985. Our experienced in-house publishing team has developed a wide range of flexible and easy to use self-teach resources for individual learners and corporate clients all over the world.

At the time of publication, we currently offer materials for:

- **ITQ Level 1, Level 2 and Level 3**

- **New CLAIT, CLAIT Plus and CLAIT Advanced**

- **ECDL Syllabus 5.0**

- **ECDL Advanced Syllabus 2.0**

- **Start IT**

- **Skill for Life in ICT**

- **Functional Skills ICT**

- **CiA Revision Series**

- **Open Learning Guides**

- **Trainers Packs with iCourse Professional**

- **And many more...**

Previous syllabus versions are also available upon request.

We hope you have enjoyed using this guide and would love to hear your opinions about our materials. To let us know how we're doing and to get up to the minute information on our current range of products, please visit us at:

**www.ciatraining.co.uk**